THE WORLD ACCORDING TO THE MAN IN THE PUB

THE WORLD
ACCORDING TO
THE MAN
IN THE PUB

201 OF OUR FAVOURITE DUBIOUS
PUB FACTS EXPLAINED

ROBERT ANWOOD

**MARKS&
SPENCER**

This edition first published in 2006 by Ebury Press,
a division of the Random House Group Limited, for Marks and Spencer p.l.c.

www.marksandspencer.com

ISBN 0091916690

Printed and bound in Great Britain by
Cox and Wyman Ltd, Reading, Berkshire

CONTENTS

'There's meaning in thy snores.'

– Sebastian, Act II Scene 1,
The Tempest, William Shakespeare

INTRODUCTION

BEFORE YOU READ ANY FURTHER, it's important to understand – particularly if you are a lawyer – that this is not a book of facts. Facts, on their own, are tedious. This is a book of *pub facts*, which are altogether a different matter, though you may come to find them equally tedious.

To enter the world of the pub fact is to enter the world of the pub itself, inside which anyone who's had a couple of pints suddenly becomes the foremost authority on any subject of their choosing. Just because the man in the pub happens to be a plumber by day is no reason why he cannot make detailed pronouncements about evolutionary theory; and the woman arguing at the bar does not require a degree in astronomy to be an expert on the workings of the solar system. Expressed with sufficient confidence, the most improbable and inaccurate statements can be made to carry the full force of *fact*. Indeed, there are those who believe strongly that any pub fact should be accompanied by a determined stabbing of the table (or bar) with the index finger, whilst exclaiming 'FACT!'

Pub facts should not be confused with trivia, although some of the items in this book overlap to a certain extent. Pure trivia lends itself to dry lists of largely unmemorable facts about the world's longest, smallest or – insert superlative here – people and places:

the kind of facts that are designed for an eyebrow-raising, 'Would you believe it?' reaction. Although not as concrete as actual, trivial facts, pub facts aren't usually as blatantly untrue as urban myths, either – although I have felt obliged to include a few classics of that genre for the sake of completeness. The defining characteristic of the pub fact is that it combines just the slightest degree of believability with a wholly unlikely claim that cannot actually be tested in the pub environment. Hence pub facticians cannot be proved or disproved – unless, of course, they whip out this book while waiting for the next round to arrive.

I have not invented the 'facts' presented here; they are merely absurd claims and extraordinary assertions that I have overheard during long periods of time wasted in the pub. Out of my own frustration, disbelief, cynicism and – let's be honest – boredom, I found myself compelled to investigate them in detail. The resulting conclusions are collected together here as a reference for anyone wanting to enhance their pub status by quoting an 'authority'.

To help you find your way through the jungle of misinformation, I have divided my investigations into broad subject areas – areas that are just as vague as the pub facts themselves. NATURE is the starting-point for novices: the natural world contains all manner of weird and wonderful creatures and curiosities, with which the careful pub-fact user can have a field day. SHOWBIZ, meanwhile, is an opportunity to juxtapose very real people with very unreal assertions. SCIENCE demonstrates what happens when knowledge is released from the lab and allowed to cross-breed with theories that are every bit as 'fuzzy' as the minds of those who espouse them. THE LAW transcends the institutions and national boundaries pedantically respected by narrow-minded, stuffed-shirt solicitors, and instead represents the true order of things — the way 'the law' simply works. The pub facts presented in HISTORY are so ill-informed that they represent the most revisionist approach to historical study of recent times; while reading the section on SPORTS gives you the equivalent health benefits of a vigorous ten-minute workout without having to leave the bar. Finally, GEOGRAPHY is where I have chosen to collect everything that wouldn't fit into any of the subject areas above, wide-ranging though they are. This is something of a tribute to my dimly remembered schooldays, when Geography seemed to be a catch-all subject: quite what oxbow lakes and Third World life expectancy could possibly have in common is beyond me, but ever since, I have thought of 'Geography' as a bogus term to describe 'stuff in general'.

My research into these 'facts' was at times fascinating, inform-ing, surprising and entertaining. But mostly it was boring and exasperating, so I congratulate you on taking the short cut in buying this book and saving yourself the trouble. Numerous individuals and institutions assisted me in the difficult process of separating the rubbish from the reality (see Acknowledgements, p. 280), but any errors that remain are entirely down to me. If there are places where I've got the wrong end of the shtick, maybe you'd be kind enough to let me know via my website, at www.robertanwood.com. Needless to say, you are not advised to use this book for backing up suspect insurance claims; as a sur-vival handbook; or to 'wow' the judge during your libel hearing.

Cheers.

Robert Anwood
May 2006

NATURE

A crocodile can run faster than a racehorse

CROCODILE, ALLIGATOR – YOU CHOOSE. But in the world of the pub fact, two things hold true: first, they can run faster than racehorses; and second, if you find yourself being chased by one, you can baffle them by running away in a zig-zag.

Crocodiles and alligators are certainly capable of exceptionally sudden bursts of speed when it comes to snatching prey. For brief flashes of speed, they can attain the equivalent of 40 kph (roughly 25 mph), but this is effectively in a single jump or a lunge from the water, which doesn't count as running and is instantaneous. In other words, after the first leap this speed could not possibly be maintained.

In terms of moving over land, croc boffins have categorised three styles: the belly crawl or belly run, the high walk and the gallop. With the belly run, top speeds have been clocked at 14 kph (9 mph) in an escape scenario. The high walk is usually pretty slow, at most 5 kph (3 mph). The gallop is the fastest of the three, though only a few species are capable of it, with the fastest accurately measured speed being 17 kph (11 mph) in a 1982 study.

Racehorses and averagely fit humans are faster — over longer distances, too. The fastest racehorse ever recorded was Big Racket, who reached just over 69 kph (43 mph) in Mexico City in 1945. So, if you're a human, just run away from the animal's habitat as quickly and directly as possible. If you're a horse, do the same, but maybe jump over a couple of hedges just to make sure.

VERDICT: FALSE

In August 2005 the fastest *pantomime* horse — two blokes inside a horse costume — reached the astonishing speed of 26.6 kph (16.5 mph) over 100 metres.

The daddy-longlegs is deadly poisonous to humans, but its mouth is so small that it cannot pierce human skin

CONFUSINGLY, THE TERM 'daddy-longlegs' describes three different creatures. In the UK, daddy-longlegs are usually crane flies (the Tipulidae family); in the US, they are normally harvestmen (the Opiliones order); but in both regions and elsewhere they can also be daddy-longlegs *spiders*, otherwise known as cellar spiders, house spiders or vibrating spiders (the Pholcidae family). Needless to say, they all have long legs (though they're not all daddies).

Another point of confusion is that some pub-fact claimants will mention mouth size, while others cite fang length or jaw strength. Others go all-out and refer to the daddy-longlegs as 'the most poisonous spider in the world'. Neither harvestmen nor crane flies have venom glands, so the latter claim clearly cannot be true for these two candidates – and neither of them are spiders, since they don't belong to the Araneae order of arachnids.

Pholcidae, which are 'actual spiders', do have venom glands, and they have a very small uncate fang structure, meaning that the fang meets a secondary tooth in a tiny pincer movement. For some reason, possibly related to muscle strength, daddy-longlegs spiders virtually never bite humans – perhaps because they're used to trapping their prey in a web before biting, unlike brown recluse spiders (*Loxosceles reclusa*), which have a similar fang structure and mouth size, and are better known for their human-biting habits.

Ultimately, there is not a single case in the medical literature of a daddy-longlegs spider's venom being fatal to humans, either by natural biting or in laboratory-based venom extraction and analysis. In other words, you're far more likely to incur a fatal 'sports injury' from batting a daddy-longlegs around the room with a rolled-up newspaper.

VERDICT: FALSE

More likely contenders for the 'most venomous spider' accolade include the funnel-web spider and the Brazilian wandering spider.

There's a type of penguin called the Macaroni

THIS IS ENTIRELY TRUE; and of all the penguins in the world, the Macaroni – *Eudyptes chrysolophus* – is the most populous, if not the most recognisable. (They have a bit of an image problem, because they look a lot like Royal penguins.)

Penguins are not generally known for their resemblance to thin tubes of pasta, so it will come as no surprise to learn that the name has a different origin. In the late 1700s, the derogatory term 'Macaroni' was used in Britain to denote a dandy 'affecting Continental fashions'. In fact, the word probably had more specifically homosexual overtones, suggesting a young man who had been to Italy on a Grand Tour and brought back louche morals and an effeminate dress sense. (Note for American readers: a Grand Tour was the eighteenth-century equivalent of *National Lampoon's European Vacation*.) This usage of the word may derive from the plural of the Italian *maccherone*, which came to mean 'fool' or 'dimwit', or it may simply have been connected with the dandies' love of Italian food.

Being a hardcore Macaroni was all about wearing a preposterously large wig with a tiny cap perched on top, decorated with bright feathers. This is alluded to in the song 'Yankee Doodle Dandy', which satirises the gauche colonial settler who 'stuck a feather in his cap' and 'called it macaroni', thereby thinking he was sporting finery as outré as the most foppish Englishman's headdress. And, to return to the penguins, the Macaroni name was probably inspired by their golden crests, which resembled the sort of cap that such a dandy was wont to wear.

VERDICT: TRUE

There should also be a type of dance called the Macaroni: it could be a bit like a risqué version of the Mashed Potato but with a kind of Salsa element.

All polar bears are left-handed

OF COURSE, polar bears don't exactly have 'hands', but it has long been asserted in Inuit tradition that the bears' left front paws are far stronger and more agile than their right. Indeed, it has been claimed that for camouflage purposes when hunting, the polar bear uses its weaker, right paw to cover up its black nose, while lashing out at its prey with its left paw.

Unfortunately, scientific research does not back up these claims.

Polar bears certainly do have agile left paws, but they are pretty much ambidextrous, making equal use of right and left. And while hunters in the Arctic regions may swear they've seen it, the nose-covering technique remains an anecdotal claim (about as believable as 'Aunt Patricia's colleague's husband woke up in an ice bath to discover his kidney was missing'). However, in particularly bitter weather a polar bear will sometimes curl up into a ball and cover up its nose – with either paw – because, as the only 'un-furred' part of the bear's body, the nose gives off a lot of heat (even the bear's paw pads can acquire fur).

Animals that have been found to be predominantly left-handed, left-pawed or left-clawed in scientific studies include badgers, lemurs, parrots and lobsters; but as with humans (where around ninety per cent are considered to be right-handed), a tendency does not mean that *every* member of the species is that way inclined.

VERDICT: FALSE

Most of the Muppets were left-handed, due to the way they were controlled by their right-handed puppeteers – *not* because left-handed creator Jim Henson wanted to act out a revenge fantasy on a right-handed world, as is sometimes claimed.

The elephant is the only mammal that cannot jump

IF 'JUMP' MEANS THAT A mammal propels its entire body upwards through the air without wings, then even whales can 'jump' out of the water when they breach, putting elephants to shame. More usually, jumping is associated with the use of leg muscles – so is the elephant the only mammal with legs that cannot jump?

Actually, *can* elephants jump? Aside from a few unverified anecdotal claims, it seems that adult elephants can't. This isn't so much to do with 'having four knees', or their adherence to a snooker-style 'one foot must always be on the floor' rule, but a simple matter of strength compared to body weight. Then again, elephants don't really *need* to jump. Having virtually no natural predators, if they come to the edge of a ravine it's not like anything will be in hot pursuit. So, they might as well take the scenic route.

Next, though, are there any other mammals that have legs but can't jump? Sloths, in keeping with their eponymous lazy image, cannot jump. Maybe now it's time to amend the claim to: 'The elephant is the only ground-based mammal with legs that cannot jump.' However, sloths do visit the forest floor periodically. Then there are hippos and rhinos, neither of which can properly jump, for the same reason that elephants can't. However, if a round of drinks is at stake in a pub argument, you could desperately try to argue that, while trotting at speed, hippos and rhinos can have all four feet off the ground at the same time, unlike elephants.

VERDICT: FALSE
In the 1980 feature-length cartoon *Animalympics*, which surely counts as scientific evidence, elephants are shown weightlifting, playing cricket and even pole-vaulting – but when it comes to launching themselves from the ground under their own steam for the hurdles or the long jump, they're nowhere to be seen.

A rat can give birth to twelve other rats every four weeks

THE TWO MAIN SPECIES OF RAT are the black rat (*Rattus rattus*, almost as well named as the gorilla – see p. 36) and the brown rat (*Rattus norvegicus*, named after The Stranglers' first album). The ones kept as pets are brown rats; so are virtually all the ones you see scuttling around sewers, litter and undergrowth, if that's the sort of environment you hang around in.

Rats have a lifespan of between two and four years, and can become pregnant after about six weeks – although for domestic breeding purposes, the advice is to wait until the female ('doe, a rat, a female rat') is at least four months old before letting it loose on ladies' nights. The gestation period is around 22 days, following which time the doe may give birth to anything from one to twenty mini-rats, or kittens. The average litter is around twelve, which may or may not be related to the fact that the doe has twelve nipples.

Here's the scary bit ('scary' if you don't like rats; 'profitable' if you're in the rat-catching trade): the doe can conceive again within a day or so of giving birth. That's not to say this sort of behaviour should be encouraged – but left to their own devices, rats aren't noted for their abstinence or sensible precautions.

Therefore, it *is* possible for a rat to give birth to twelve kittens every four weeks (although rats that become pregnant again so soon after birth may have a longer gestation). Breeding at full throttle, a single pair of rats could then be responsible for 156 immediate children in the course of a year; and if half of those were females and propagated at the same rate, that would make, er . . . a lot of rats – exactly how many would depend on whether they interbred and had twelfty kittens each or received a new influx of 'love rats' from other colonies.

VERDICT: TRUE

According to the National Pest Technicians Association, the UK brown rat population 'supersized' itself by 34 per cent between 1998 and 2003, mainly due to massive over-snacking on discarded burgers, kebabs and chips.

Camels have three eyelids

DROMEDARIES HAVE ONE HUMP, Bactrians have two – but both species have three eyelids per eye. Two of the eyelids function in the same way as human eyelids: opening and closing vertically for the purposes of cleaning the eye; shutting out bright light; protecting against airborne particles, water or other irritants; and fluttering bashfully when coaxing middle-aged men into lapses of judgement, like ignoring lost train tickets or opening high-security bank vaults.

What camels have – in common with crocodiles, birds and some other mammals – is a 'third eyelid' in the form of a nictitating membrane, sometimes called the haw. This translucent membrane, underneath the outer eyelids, slides horizontally across the eye to protect it, but lets through sufficient light for a camel to see roughly where it's going even in the middle of a sandstorm. Other features camels have developed for keeping out sand include a double

row of long lashes on their outer eyelids, and the ability to close their nostrils fully.

In other animals, nictitating membranes act like goggles. In the case of polar bears they help to avoid snow blindness, while beavers use them to see better when swimming underwater.

VERDICT: TRUE

Camel wrestling is a big sport in parts of Turkey where, according to the Ministry of Culture and Tourism, it's common to name camels after the cigar-chomping TV detective Columbo.

Some snakes hear through their tongues

'SOME' SNAKES? Which ones? It's a suitably vague claim that doesn't involve knowing anything about different types of snakes or their physiological make-up.

Until quite recently ophiologists – snake scientists – used to believe that snakes could not 'hear' sound waves carried through the air, and scoffed at snake-charmers for being con artists when it came to playing flutes. It was originally thought that snakes could only sense vibrations from the surface they were travelling on – so if you were to stamp on the ground near a snake, it would feel the movement in the earth. However, it's now known that they can hear airborne sounds as well.

Snakes don't have external ears, channelling sound from the outside like human ears, but they do have inner ears. Vibrations from the ground may be passed through the snake's jaw to the inner ears by way of a small bone called the columella. Airborne sounds are also transmitted through the snake's body to the inner ears, but they don't specifically 'hear through their tongues'.

They do, however, *smell* through their tongues. Particles collected on the tongue are inserted into the two pits of an organ (the vomeronasal organ, or Jacobson's organ) on the roof of the snake's mouth that effectively detects odours. The forks – or should that be 'tines'? – of the tongue therefore allow snakes to smell in stereo and figure out whether they should go left or right to pick up their lunch.

VERDICT: FALSE
Snakes can't crawl backwards, in case you were wondering.

A mouse can fit through a hole the size of a biro

DURING WARMER MONTHS, the common house mouse (the brawny-sounding *Mus musculus*) is content to live outdoors, eating cereal grains and seeds. But at the first sign of a cold snap, they'll scamper towards the nearest human dwelling and find their way in. Once they get there, they abandon any pretence of healthy eating, and will nibble at (but not necessarily consume) practically anything they can get their tiny teeth on, including lead, rubber, plastic and some forms of concrete: they have to gnaw all the time, to keep their ever-growing incisors trimmed. Contrary to cartoon lore, like Mel Blanc's attitude to carrots (see p. 57), mice don't 'especially' like cheese.

It's this gnawing, along with a relatively soft skull and an already slender body, that allows the mouse to get through improbably small holes. Any openings in your home wider than about 6 millimetres (a quarter of an inch) and you're in trouble – through a combination of squeezing and snacking, the mouse and its extended family, beer buddies and associated hangers-on will be moving in and partying hard for the foreseeable future. So your best line of defence against mice is quite simple, though tedious: seal up any and all small openings. Be aware, however, that the action-hero mouse can also jump 46 centimetres (18 inches) vertically upwards, swim, travel upside down and climb up pretty much anything.

The reason why biros (ballpoint pens) and pencils are often cited is that they're everyday household items with which to usefully check openings – if the biro will fit, so will a mouse.

VERDICT: TRUE

One mouse that can't fit through a hole the size of a biro is a breed on Gough Island in the South Atlantic, where *one million* seabird chicks – albatrosses, petrels, shearwaters and Gough buntings – are being eaten alive each year by supermice that grow to three times the size of normal house mice.

If you cut off a cockroach's head, it can live for several weeks, only dying due to starvation

IN THE WORLD OF PUB BIOLOGY, the cockroach must be the hardest animal around, being able – supposedly – to survive a nuclear holocaust. The latter is actually a moot point: cockroaches have a tolerance to radiation some fifteen times higher than humans, so although they could survive the after-effects of a nuclear attack, they couldn't withstand the initial blast if they were in the vicinity at the time.

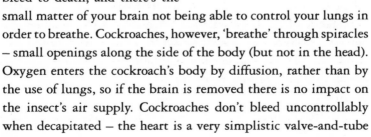

When it comes to losing one's head, there are a couple of reasons why it's fairly problematic for humans and other mammals. For example, there's the severing of the carotid arteries and other vessels, meaning you'd bleed to death; and there's the small matter of your brain not being able to control your lungs in order to breathe. Cockroaches, however, 'breathe' through spiracles – small openings along the side of the body (but not in the head). Oxygen enters the cockroach's body by diffusion, rather than by the use of lungs, so if the brain is removed there is no impact on the insect's air supply. Cockroaches don't bleed uncontrollably when decapitated – the heart is a very simplistic valve-and-tube contraption – although the wound can become infected; and they can go for about a month without food if they remain in cool surroundings, providing they've been allowed some sort of 'last supper' just before the beheading (ideally a huge bucket of ice cream).

Weirder still, a decapitated cockroach won't just sit around chilling out. The nervous system of a cockroach is less centralised than a human's, and stimulation of ganglia on the cockroach's abdomen can cause a headless cockroach to scuttle away from any unsportsmanlike predator.

VERDICT: TRUE
In short, a cockroach won't be getting the role of an Immortal in the next *Highlander* movie.

One dog year equals seven human years

SOME HUMANS LIVE longer than others and the same goes for dogs. Pooch pundits have calculated that overall, in developed countries, dogs have a life expectancy of about 12.8 years on average. The smaller the breed, the longer they live: proof that the best things come in small packages. (Disclaimer: packaging dogs is probably illegal and should not be attempted.) It's bad news for the Irish wolfhound – the tallest breed – which is lucky to make it beyond six years; and good news for the ever-amusing shih-tzu, which can look forward to nearly 13.5 years of relentless stick-chasing.

It's often claimed that seven years of human life equate to one year of a dog's. At first sight, this seems excessive: an average canine lifetime of 12.8 years works out at 89.6 human years, whereas human life expectancy in developed countries is nearer to 78 (although if you happen to live in Andorra, you can expect to make it to about 83.5).

The main reason the calculation is bogus, however, is that no kind of linear conversion can be applied, since dogs and humans age at different rates at different times in their lives. Generally, by the time they reach one year of age, dogs have almost fully 'grown up' and sexually matured, which could equate to something nearer fifteen human years. So dogs develop more quickly by comparison, becoming fully mature within about a tenth (or less) of their overall life span, whereas humans fully mature within about a fifth of theirs (unless you're a character in a Robin Williams film). Which means that dogs have a very short childhood and probably a very long mid-life crisis.

VERDICT: BARKING UP THE WRONG TREE
Studies have shown that humans who keep pets live longer (than other humans, not just their pets).

Goats have rectangular pupils

IT'S EASY TO ASSUME THAT all animals have circular pupils like those of humans; but you only have to look at a cat to see that its pupil is a vertical slit that can pretty much close completely. By contrast, goats (and most other hoofed animals) have horizontal slits, which in the right light look rectangular.

So what are the consequences of having rectangular pupils?

Goats have a field of vision between 320° and 340°, meaning that they can see virtually all around them, in every direction, without moving. But extent of vision is primarily related to the position of the eyes in the head, rather than the shape of the pupil: hares, for example, have 360° vision, while humans have a field of vision between 160° and 210°. Position of the eyes – and probably the lack of anything you could call a neck – explains why pigs can't look up (and neither can dogs, according to Big Al in the film *Shaun of the Dead*). Meanwhile, horses can apparently look straight behind them but not straight ahead.

As for pupil shape, having a non-circular pupil means that the iris muscles can close the aperture more fully, with the result that less light gets to the retina. The eyes of animals like cats and goats tend to be able to let in more light than other animals, giving them much better night-time vision; but the shape of their pupils allows them to contract their irises more fully during daylight, meaning that they can effectively catch mice – or blades of grass – 24 hours a day.

VERDICT: TRUE

Like goats and other ungulates, octopuses have rectangular pupils; then again, octopuses also have beaks. Weird.

The hippopotamus is the most dangerous animal in Africa

BY 'DANGEROUS', ONE WOULD ASSUME that 'animal killing the most humans' is the award being handed out here, rather than 'animal most liable to render buildings structurally unsound' – and that humans themselves don't count as animals in this contest. The mosquito is responsible for millions of deaths every year (see p. 149) but unlike the hippo, the mosquito's danger factor is indirect.

Make my day, Punk

At first sight hippos appear to be lardy, harmless beasts who spend all day dozing in the water, but the unpredictable three-ton mammals are actually lean, mean killing machines (not to be confused with George Foreman's Lean Mean Grilling Machines). They lash out, making use of their considerable bulk, sharp tusks and incredibly strong jaw muscles, for the purposes of seizing food, winning 'ownership' of females (in the case of bulls), protecting their calves (in the case of cows) and staking territorial claims. Most adult males are covered in scars from battles with other bulls, and some have been known to kill calves in order to gain renewed mating rights with the mother – not the most convincing of pulling techniques.

Normally full-on herbivores, some hippos have been known to feast on impala and even their own kind. However, they don't kill humans for food, but primarily to protect territory, with a common strategy being to capsize a boat and then attack its occupants.

Unfortunately for fact-debunkers, there are no reliable animal-attack figures relating to the whole of Africa. Ironically there are plenty of statistics about the number of hippos killed by humans each year.

VERDICT: UNPROVEN BUT CREDIBLE

The most dangerous *individual* animal in Africa may be a 6-metre (20-foot) crocodile called Gustave, which lives in Burundi, has killed more than 300 people, and once ate a whole adult hippo.

A polar bear's fur is actually colourless

POLAR BEARS HAVE COMPLETELY BLACK SKIN. For inhabitants of the icy north, this is a serious problem if you obtain your food by creeping up on unsuspecting seals – unless, that is, your skin happens to be camouflaged by thick, white fur, also highly effective in keeping you warm.

A big ball of white fuzz is certainly the traditional image of the polar bear (optionally swigging on a bottle of Coke), but at sunset and sunrise they may actually appear to be a yellowy-orange colour. This is because a polar bear's hair is a dense fur of transparent, colourless strands, so in particularly intense coloured light it will appear to take on that hue. In normal daytime conditions, owing to the way the daylight reflects, it appears white, providing the fur is clean. A polar bear's fur is cleanest and hence whitest just after it has moulted, towards the end of summer. By contrast, at the end of winter the bear's fur is likely to be a pretty manky shade of what might politely be described as 'eggshell white'.

Another factor affecting the colour of the polar bear is the hollow, tube-like nature of its outer hairs, with gunk often getting stuck in them. In Singapore Zoo in 2004, two polar bears, Sheba and her son Inuka – who was the first polar bear to be born and bred in the tropics – turned green because of algae in the hollow parts of their hair. The algae was harmless, but to avoid any more 'bad fur days' the zookeepers bleached it out.

VERDICT: TRUE

The 'fibre optics' theory, in which the hollow hairs are said to funnel heat to the polar bear's body (with the black skin more readily absorbing it), is totally unfounded.

The world's termites outweigh the world's humans by 10 to 1

TERMITES DON'T FILL in census forms (though if they did, they would probably claim to belong to the Jedi religion for a laugh), so any estimate of the world's termite population must be a wildly vague guess. However, we do know quite a bit about how these social insects live: in colonies ranging from a village (a few hundred termites) to a metropolis (a million or more termites).

Similarly, while estimates of the world's human population are relatively accurate, any estimation of the overall *weight* of humans will be pretty arbitrary. So the whole comparison is destined to end in an unverifiable, inconclusive and useless measurement that will carry no validity whatsoever. What the heck, let's do it anyway.

By February 2006, the human population had officially reached 6.5 billion. Taking into account all age ranges, let's guesstimate the average human weight (or technically, mass) to be 50 kilograms (about 110 pounds). That's a total human biomass of a lardy 325 million metric tons.

For the next made-up statistic, let's say that your average termite weighs about 10 milligrams, because a round 10 makes it easier to multiply and divide. If the world's termite population outweighs humans by 10 to 1, the total termite population must weigh at least 3.25 billion metric tons. Dividing 3.25 billion metric tons by 10 milligrams gives us an estimated global termite population of 325 quadrillion critters.

So, is that a plausible number? A 1982 study by P.R. Zimmerman *et al.* in the journal *Science* – examining the effects of termite-generated methane in the earth's atmosphere – gives the world's termite population as 240 quadrillion, which is about three-quarters of the figure estimated here, suggesting that, if the calculations are accurate (which they are not, in any sense), the world's termites outweigh the world's humans by about 7.5 to 1. It could be closer to 10 to 1 if the termite population has increased at a similar rate to the human population since 1982.

VERDICT: UNVERIFIABLE, INCONCLUSIVE AND USELESS
Termites are most closely related to cockroaches, even though the word 'termite' comes from the Latin *termes*, meaning 'woodworm'.

Rats can't vomit, or else they would die

VOMITING CAN BE defined as the involuntary ejection of the stomach contents through the mouth, resulting from the reflexive contraction of abdominal muscles – as distinguished from regurgitation, which is the controlled or passive movement of partially digested food back up into the mouth, a technique used by many birds to feed their young. Rats have occasionally been known to regurgitate and to choke while eating, but they can't vomit. This is why you never see a rat hunched over an open sewer, yakking up while another rat holds its whiskers back. It doesn't matter how much gunk you feed them or how many Robin Williams movies you make them sit through – they simply can't throw up. In fact, they can't even burp. This is because of a 'limiting ridge' between the two parts of a rat's stomach and the rat's inability to coordinate the operation of the diaphragm muscles involved.

Just because an animal cannot vomit (neither can guinea pigs or rabbits, incidentally) doesn't mean that it would die if it did.

The whole point about vomiting is that it's reflexive – so a rat can't *choose* whether to vomit or not, with the wrong choice having catastrophic consequences. Similarly, the suggestion that rats have ever died because they were about to vomit is ridiculous.

Rats' inability to vomit makes them especially susceptible to poisoning by humans. In terms of avoiding toxins, their approach is to pick fussily at a small amount of food to start with. If it seems okay, they scoff the rest later. If it made them feel queasy (although they can't throw up, they can experience nausea), rats are fast learners with keen senses of taste and smell, and the chances are they will successfully avoid the substance in future. Another rat strategy for dealing with dodgy food is to eat clay, which effectively 'soaks up' and neutralises some toxins – a bit like the fried breakfast a hungover human might eat, although not as tasty or greasy.

VERDICT: TRUE, APART FROM THE 'OR ELSE THEY WOULD DIE' BIT
Honey is made from nectar, which bees repeatedly puke up from a special 'honey stomach'.

You can't smell while you're asleep

YOU'VE PROBABLY EXPERIENCED 'hearing' strange sounds in your dreams that, upon waking up, turn out to be noises invading from the real world – an alarm clock, the radio, a partner's stentorian snoring, or the boss hammering on the front door to find out why you haven't been at work for the last four hours. But who can remember *smelling* something during a dream? Well, some people can.

It's often claimed in relation to smoke that you can't smell while you're asleep. According to this argument, because the sense of smell is non-existent while you're asleep, you cannot safely rely on your brain waking you up when smoke fumes enter the room. Numerous studies have found that, while the sense of smell will certainly wake up most people in the early stages of sleep, during deep sleep smoke odours will wake up some people and not others. In other words, you should certainly fit a smoke alarm rather than rely on being woken by the smell of burning – but that's not to say that no one can smell while they're asleep.

Back in 1899, Hiram M. Stanley reported in an article called 'Artificial Dreams' the effects of wafting heliotropes around under a sleeping person's nose, which caused the sleeper to dream about flying on an airship through a snowstorm, over a country 'covered with white enamel and filled with white elephants' – apparently a characteristic of opium dreams. Which makes you wonder about cheese dreams: you shouldn't eat cheese before you go to bed, because it'll give you nightmares; but what if you can *smell* something pungent like Roquefort as well? No one wants to see cheese elephants.

VERDICT: FALSE

Some studies have found that people who said they couldn't smell certain odours while awake were actually affected by those same odours while they were asleep – this could be an important olfactory phenomenon, or perhaps the paid volunteers were just lying in order to string out the experiment for as long as possible.

If you're being chased by a bear, you should run downhill

THIS IS A WIDELY ACCEPTED escape strategy, based on the premise that bears can't run downhill. You don't need to have been anywhere near a grizzly to be convinced about the truth of this physical limitation; indeed, many an armchair explorer will claim that it is part of standard-issue US military guidelines for procedure in the wild. (Clearly, US soldiers often come face-to-snout with bears in combat situations.) The claim may have

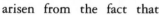

arisen from the fact that bears have shorter front legs than back legs, suggesting that they would stumble like a cow with foot-and-mouth when trying to run downhill.

This is patently false. Bears can run fast over any kind of terrain, both uphill and downhill, at speeds of up to 48 kph (about 30 mph) –

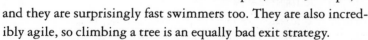

and they are surprisingly fast swimmers too. They are also incredibly agile, so climbing a tree is an equally bad exit strategy.

According to experts, the best tactic is actually to remain calm, speak in a low voice (presumably in any language) or wave your hands slowly, while backing away from the bear's 'personal space'.

When the bear realises you are a human – evidently our clothing and brightly coloured rucksacks do not always give the game away – it will probably back away first in any case. Another advantage of this approach is that you don't have to rely on the luck of being already uphill before you encounter the bear.

VERDICT: DEBUNKED!

However, it is true that cows can't walk downstairs.

Guinea pigs can't sweat

YOU'VE PROBABLY FIGURED out by now that guinea pigs aren't pigs, and they don't come from Guinea. Exactly how they acquired their moniker – being rodents that come from the Andes, where they provide a protein-rich food source – is the subject of much speculation, with the *Oxford English Dictionary*'s best guess being that they may have been compared to young guinea hogs (which *are* hogs and *do* come from Guinea).

Guinea pigs, referred to as 'cavies' by people who take guinea pigs seriously, don't have sweat glands. This means they can overheat quite easily in warm surroundings and suffer problems relating to fluid retention, so if you keep guinea pigs, it's important to keep them cool. Since the most energetic thing they're likely to do is 'popcorn' (a funky little jump accompanied by a squeak), they're unlikely to work up much heat from physical exercise alone, so you will rarely see a guinea pig wearing 1980s-style sweatbands or sitting in the corner of its cage emptying a bucket of water onto its head like an exhausted boxer.

Other animals can't sweat either, like 'actual' pigs and rabbits. But don't think about putting rabbits and guinea pigs together (in the hope that they'll bond over stories about remaining perfectly cool and dry under stress) because the chances are the guinea pig will be either attacked or lusted after by the other rodent.

VERDICT: TRUE

In Peru's Cuzco Cathedral there is a painting of the Last Supper by Marcos Zapata, in which Jesus and his disciples are about to chow down on a roast guinea pig – a scene that is about as historically watertight as *The Da Vinci Code*.

The scientific name for the gorilla is *Gorilla gorilla gorilla*

THE SCIENTIFIC CLASSIFICATION of gorillas has changed in recent years, as primatologists have understood more about their physical characteristics and geographical distribution. Once thought to be a single species with three sub-species, they are now usually divided into two separate species of the genus *Gorilla*: Eastern gorillas and Western gorillas, each with its own sub-species. According to Greek texts from around the fifth century BC, the word that was subsequently transported to English as 'gorilla' was an African name for a wild or hairy man.

The Eastern gorilla's species name is *beringei*, while the Western gorilla is simply *gorilla*. It's when you list the sub-species name together with the genus and species names (rather than just the binomial name at the species level) that things start to get really confusing.

On the Eastern side, the mountain gorilla's sub-species name is also *beringei*, so its full classification is *Gorilla beringei beringei*, while the Eastern lowland gorilla is *Gorilla beringei graueri*. There is also a possible third sub-species of Eastern gorilla called the Bwindi gorilla. This hasn't yet been formally identified and conferred with a sub-species name, so scientifically speaking it might as well be Murdoc Niccals.

As for the Western gorillas, there is the critically endangered Cross River gorilla, *Gorilla gorilla diehli*, and finally the Western lowland gorilla – which really is so good they named it thrice: *Gorilla gorilla gorilla*. Since the Western lowland gorilla is the most common sub-species by a long way, with a population of about 100,000 compared to nearer 5,000 for the Eastern lowland gorilla and around only 500 for the remaining sub-species, it seems reasonable to judge this fact to be basically true.

VERDICT: TRUE, FOR THE MOST PART
Gorillas laugh when tickled.

If pigeons eat rice they explode

THIS FACT IS OFTEN ACCOMPANIED by a warning not to throw rice at weddings because pigeons (and other birds) will eat it, causing their digestive systems to swell up and explode. Given that many churches handle several weddings a day, this claim can be swiftly discounted on the basis that no one has ever arrived at a ceremony to find the staff hastily sweeping up piles of feathers, beaks and gizzards. In reality, venues that discourage the throwing of rice do so because it's a faff to clean up, and also because it's a health and safety nightmare due to the slapstick 'slip hazard' represented by thousands of grains of rice strewn over the church steps. You may as well empty out a bucket of ball-bearings while you're at it, then stand back and put the video camera on standby for the inevitable *You've Been Framed* clip.

The supposed 'science' behind the assertion is that the uncooked rice expands up to three or four times its original volume when soaked in water, which in this case would be swilling around a bird's insides. Therefore, if a lot is pecked up in a very short space of time, the pigeon would be unable to process the rice grains quickly enough, resulting in the explosion. But by this logic, there's no reason to restrict the fact to birds – it sounds similar to the 'rice torture' force-feeding technique that, according to generations of scaremongering British schoolchildren, is used on humans in China. (Schoolchildren in China probably allege that in Britain, 'they' torture people by force-feeding them Yorkshire pudding.)

Aside from anecdotal and unverifiable claims, there is no real evidence of pigeons or other animals overindulging on rice to an explosive extent, which makes this a classic urban myth.

VERDICT: FALSE

This myth was perpetuated by advice columnist Ann Landers at least twice during her career, earning rebukes from the USA Rice Federation.

Butterflies taste with their feet

THE BUTTERFLY IS the pub factician's dream creature: it's amazing that this humble insect hasn't been crushed to extinction under the astonishing weight of trivia it supports.

Butterflies smell with their antennae. They don't have lungs. They have green blood. Then there's that whole metamorphosis business. Some of them can fly as fast as 48 kph (30 mph). Last but not least, they taste with their feet. (Some can also, in fact, taste with their ovipositor – that bit at the back used to lay eggs.)

Tasting with their feet, or more accurately their tarsi, means they can easily make snap decisions about whether any given plant might be suitable for laying eggs or finding nectar. Clearly a benefit, until you accidentally land on a bowl of peanuts (see p. 119) – in which case, you're probably looking at a severe example of chaos theory.

While butterflies do taste with their feet, they tend to eat (or rather drink) in a slightly more conventional manner, through their proboscis – if they have one, that is: some butterflies have nothing like a mouth at all, and have to rely for survival on food stores built up when they were a caterpillar. This seems a little unfair, unless they are genetically pre-programmed to 'know' that they won't have a mouth when they grow up.

VERDICT: TRUE

The monarch butterfly's feet are approximately two thousand times more sensitive than a human tongue.

A swan can break a man's arm

'MY GRANDFATHER ONCE SAW a man's arm broken by a swan' – this kind of tale is all well and good, but it's a tricky one to test in the field. Coercing a swan to take part in such an experiment is likely to result in a visit from the police, while you'd have to search for at least two hours to find a meth-addled *Jackass* fan stupid enough to risk a waterbird-inflicted arm-snapping.

The first person to popularise this classic pub fact may have been the bird-fancier John James Audubon, who catalogued and painted the feathered fauna of North America during the nineteenth century, and who on one occasion believed that a Canada goose had broken his arm (though this turned out to be a stereotypically male exaggeration of a slight graze). In Audubon's best-selling book *Birds of America* (which sounds like a travel guide written for British lads out on the pull in the States) he cites the improbably named Dr Sharpless, who claimed, without any particular substantiating evidence, that a large swan is 'more than a match for a man in four feet of water, a stroke of the wing having broken an arm'. Dr Sharpless also said that a swan will 'readily beat off a dog' – so make of his testimony what you will.

Swans can be very protective of their young, and in addition to hissing and snapping they will fend off intruders with their wings, which are both strong and large, with a span of up to 2.75 metres (about 9 feet). In 2001, a twelve-year-old boy suffered a broken leg as a result of provoking a swan on the River Foyle in Northern Ireland, and along the same stretch of river the following year a second youngster had his arm broken by another swan (or perhaps it was the same one). Adolescents count as 'young men', which is surely just about sufficient to prove this claim.

VERDICT: TRUE

Chris Tarrant, presenter of the British version of *Who Wants To Be a Millionaire?*, is rumoured to have been thrown out of Birmingham University for stealing and cooking a swan from the university lake.

Caterpillars have false legs

WHILE THE TOTAL NUMBER of legs – false or otherwise – of different types of caterpillar vary, they all have three pairs of legs attached to the three segments of the thorax. These jointed legs are what become the six legs of the butterfly following metamorphosis.

In addition to the six real legs, caterpillars also have up to five pairs of 'prolegs', or false legs, attached to the segments of the abdomen. The false legs are stumpy and not jointed, and typically end in lots of miniature hooks or crochets, whose function is often compared to that of Velcro, although much quieter.

Armed with this knowledge, fans of Eric Carle's classic picture-book *The Very Hungry Caterpillar* may be distraught to notice that it is depicted on the iconic cover with a rather arbitrary set of four legs (or perhaps four pairs of legs) at the front and two legs (or pairs of legs) at the back. Then again, the caterpillar in question eats its way through a bewildering selection of food including (on Saturday alone) one piece of chocolate cake, one ice-cream cone, one pickle, one slice of Swiss cheese, one slice of salami, one lollipop, one piece of cherry pie, one sausage, one cupcake, and one slice of watermelon – so a realistic portrayal was probably not uppermost in Eric Carle's mind.

The word 'caterpillar' is said by some to derive from the Old Northern French word *chatepelose*, meaning 'hairy cat', although this origin has not been definitively established. Certainly it can't have been its multiple legs that would cause a cigarette-sized insect to be mistaken for a feline. And aren't cats hairy anyway?

VERDICT: TRUE

There's a kind of caterpillar called the woolly bear; the number of brown hairs on its body can supposedly indicate the harshness of the coming winter.

Bears are descended from whales

(Creationists: look away now.)

THIS SOUNDS LIKE THE SORT OF fact that might have been invented by Ian Brown out of The Stone Roses, who once sang that 'dolphins were monkeys that didn't like the land'. Are bears simply whales that didn't like the sea?

Pub evolutionary theory states that at one time, sea creatures got bored and struggled out of the water to develop into today's land animals. So it seems plausible that bears descended from something aquatic – and the whale is, after all, a fellow mammal. If *this* seems faintly preposterous, consider what must have been going through Charles Darwin's head when he suggested in *The Origin of Species* that it was actually the other way round. He cited reports of North American black bears swim-

ming through the water with their mouths open, collecting insects, and concluded: 'I can see no difficulty in a race of bears being rendered, by natural selection, more and more aquatic in their structure and habits, with larger and larger mouths, till a creature was produced as monstrous as a whale.' No difficulty whatsoever.

Recent studies have found that the animal with the most similar DNA to the whale is the hippopotamus, a water-dwelling, lethal beast (see p. 27). However, to confuse matters further, it is now believed that whales and other cetaceans are not descended from hippos but from a group of land-based artiodactyls (old-skool hoofed mammals) that gave rise to camels, goats, cows, pigs and hippos. So pub evolutionary theory can be refined as follows: some creatures got bored with the ocean, turned into leaf-eating land mammals, then got bored again and went back into the water. In other words, Darwin's idea wasn't that ridiculous.

Bears, meanwhile, are actually descended from dogs. *Cephalogale* were already chasing sticks thirty million years ago, and about ten million years later (dogs are slow learners, after all), a sort of proto-bear developed, *Ursavus elemensis*.

VERDICT: FALSE

If you're trying to find Darwin's bears-to-whales claim, in the words of *This Is Spinal Tap*'s Marty DiBergi, 'don't look for it now' – he removed it from Chapter VI after the first edition due to sheer embarrassment, which in retrospect is only partly justified.

There's a type of lizard called *Chuckus norrisensis*

THERE IS NO SUCH LIZARD. Nor is it even remotely plausible that, if one were to name a reptile after grizzled action-thriller veteran Chuck Norris, it could be called *Chuckus norrisensis*, since this would suggest the creation of a new genus derived from the actor's first name, and a species derived from his last name; or perhaps a species derived from his first name, and a sub-species from his last (in which case, *Chuckus* would technically need to be lower-case — are you bored yet?). Neither possibility makes much sense.

In a similar vein, however, there *is* a dinosaur named after guitarist Mark Knopfler: *Masiakasaurus knopfleri*. The discovery of the snaggle-toothed theropod in Madagascar was announced in 2001 by a group of scientists who had spent a lot of time — one might say too much time — listening to Dire Straits while digging for fossils (rock + dinosaur = Mark Knopfler: the joke pretty much writes itself). The *Masiakasaurus* bit is a combination of the Malagasy word for 'vicious' and 'saurus' (from the Greek *sauros*) to denote a lizard — as in *Tyrannosaurus rex*, which, by a happy circular coincidence, is an example of a rock group being named after a dinosaur.

Other celebrity animal coinages include a lemur named after comic John Cleese (*Avahi cleesei*, also from Madagascar); three slime-mould beetles named after members of the George W. Bush administration (*Agathidium bushi*, *Agathidium cheneyi* and *Agathidium rumsfeldi*); a jellyfish named after Frank Zappa (*Phialella zappai*); and a single-celled sea creature named in commemoration of Queen Elizabeth II's golden jubilee (*Askenasia regina*).

VERDICT: UTTER NONSENSE

Perhaps Chuck Norris was jealous of the likes of Mark Knopfler, John Cleese, Frank Zappa and the Queen, and started this rumour out of spite.

If it can't find any food, the ribbon worm will eat itself

RIBBON WORMS, OR PROBOSCIS WORMS, belong to the phylum Nemertea (sometimes called Rhynchocoela) and are notable for two things. First, they attack prey using a proboscis that shoots out to pull food back to the worm's mouth, and which in some species has a harpoon-like attachment called a stylet, for injecting powerful neurotoxins into the unsuspecting victim. Nice. Second, while some are tiny, they can also be incredibly long – up to 30 metres (98 feet) in the case of the bootlace worm, *Lineus longissimus*. Dubious reports of specimens double that length (usually involving worms being washed ashore near St Andrew's in Scotland while someone was playing a round of golf) would suggest that the bootlace worm is the longest animal on the planet.

All nemerteans can regenerate bits of their bodies and some species reproduce asexually by fragmenting into mini-worms;

so you'd think that having a crafty self-snack shouldn't pose a problem. In terms of dining preferences, they normally prey on bristle worms, barnacles, crab eggs or fish, while one particularly extravagant species, *Cerebratulus lacteus*, feeds on clams. On occasion, nemerteans have been known to exhibit cannibalism – in other words, eating other nemerteans, but not *eating themselves*.

What would be gained by a ribbon worm – or any other animal – eating itself? Some versions of this fact specifically state that 'the ribbon worm can digest 95 per cent of its own body weight', and this probably brings us somewhere nearer the truth. Nemerteans are noted for being able to survive very long periods of time without food. During this time, they will shrink, sometimes to an incredible extent: *Prostoma rubrum* has been known to starve to just 1 per cent of its original size over the course of a rather boring year without food. (That's taking the whole 'eating is cheating' rule a bit far, really.) Consequently, the proboscis and internal organs may degenerate – but let's make this clear once and for all: *the ribbon worm is not nipping away at its own tail*.

VERDICT: FALSE

If it were true, the ribbon worm would no doubt describe itself as tasting 'a bit like chicken'.

Rice is a fruit

REFERRING TO THE plant or crop as a whole, rice is in fact a grass: the word usually refers to the species *Oryza sativa*, native to Asia, though now cultivated extensively throughout the world in numerous varieties. The word can also refer to African rice (*Oryza glaberrima*), which is gradually being displaced by *Oryza sativa* as a subsistence crop in many parts of Africa. And then there's wild rice, a group of grasses in the genus *Zizania*, closely related to 'real' rice.

In terms of what we usually eat, rice is termed a grain. However, the botany is rather complex, and if you look into it in detail, you'll probably wish you'd never asked.

The fruit of the rice plant – the caryopsis – is what contains the edible bit. A caryopsis, common to grasses, is a dry fruit in which the pericarp, or ovary wall, is fused to the coat of the single seed it contains. The caryopsis and its husk form a grain. When it comes to eating the stuff, the de-husked grain – the caryopsis itself – is what we know as brown rice: once sneered at for being rough-and-ready, but nowadays praised for its high nutritional value (file alongside brown bread). If you remove the bran layers and the germ from the caryopsis, and then give it a little polish, you end up with white rice.

So, depending which bit of the plant you're referring to, yes: rice can be a fruit, a grass and a grain. Happy now?

VERDICT: TRUE

These were just the edited highlights – you really don't want to get involved with concepts like integument, lemma, palea, rachilla, awn, tegmen, aleurone, plumule, coleophyll, mesocotyl, cotyledon, radicle, epiblast or scutellum, unless you're training for an appearance on *Countdown*.

Nutmeg is poisonous

WHAT WE GENERALLY KNOW AS 'nutmeg' is the seed from the fruit of the nutmeg tree (*Myristica fragrans*), used as a spice in cooking – although mace, another common spice, derives from the outer

casing of the same seed. If we happily go chucking nutmeg into
our mulled wine, eggnog and
soup, how can it be poisonous?

Well, it's a bit like alcohol:
consumed in small quantities
it's relatively harmless, but in
larger amounts it will lead to
some pretty bad side-effects,
such as nausea, dehydration
and leaving insulting mes-
sages on your boss's voicemail.
So when it comes to nutmeg,
how much constitutes 'binge
seasoning'?

As little as 2 grams can cause fever, headaches and effects
similar to those of amphetamines; 7.5 grams can induce con-
vulsions and muscle pain; and doses of 10 grams or more
can lead to hallucination, which is why people have been known
to ingest large amounts of nutmeg in search of a 'legal high'.
It's generally not advised, since by consuming even one whole
nutmeg seed (or the equivalent quantity of ground nutmeg)
you are risking the onset of nutmeg psychosis, a psychiatric
disorder characterised by agitation, confusion and a sensation of
imminent doom or calamity. However, there have only been two
documented fatalities resulting from nutmeg overdoses: one
was an eight-year-old boy, reported in 1908, while the other
was a 55-year-old woman in 2001 – although in her case she had
also taken flunitrazepam (more commonly known by the

proprietary name Rohypnol), which was believed to be a contributory factor.

VERDICT: TRUE
The use of nutmeg as a recreational drug is reportedly most widespread among students and prisoners – two social groups that typically have limited financial resources or restricted access to 'proper' drugs.

You shouldn't feed chocolate to dogs

DOGS ARE RENOWNED for eating absolutely anything – whether it's the remains of your Meat Feast pizza or another dog's vomit. If presented with a chocolate selection, a dog will wolf the lot, probably including the moulded plastic tray, faster than you can say 'Savoy Truffle'. But that doesn't mean they *should* eat chocolate: it just means that dogs are too stupid to recognise a coma-inducing substance when they sniff it. Which is exactly what chocolate is when it comes to canines.

The two key factors at work are theobromine and caffeine – methylxanthines that can be consumed in relatively large doses by humans without problem, but which are highly toxic in small quantities to dogs, cats and cows, among other animals. (Cats, of course, are smart; and while cows are every bit as dim-witted as dogs, they don't usually get the opportunity to go prowling round your kitchen eating everything in sight.)

Obviously, the more chocolate a dog eats in proportion to its size, the more serious the effects: a medical rule of thumb is that one ounce of milk chocolate consumed per pound of the dog's weight is enough to cause death by chocolate. Lesser effects, which may be exhibited within six hours of snacking, start with poly-dipsia (furious over-drinking), vomiting and diarrhoea, but these can be followed by seizures, hyperthermia (furious over-heating) and coma. Basically, if you find a suspicious stash of Mars Bar wrappers in your dog's kennel, you'd be well advised to call the vet as soon as possible.

VERDICT: TRUE

Grapes, raisins and macadamia nuts can also be fatal when con-sumed by dogs – although 'they' have yet to conclusively figure out why.

All the golden hamsters in the world are descended from a hamster found in Syria in 1930

YOU'D THINK THAT hamsters must be descended from at least *two* other hamsters – a male and a female. But the basis of this claim is that a mother captured in the wild, together with her litter but *not* the father, is supposedly the known ancestor of all the golden hamsters on the planet today. As bizarre as it sounds, this isn't too far from the truth.

The golden hamster (*Mesocricetus auratus*) was certainly captured in the wild prior to the twentieth century. For example, it is described by Alexander Russell, a doctor practising during the 1740s in Aleppo (in modern-day Syria), or possibly his brother Patrick, who compiled the posthumous second edition of

Alexander Russell's *The Natural History of Aleppo*. However, the bungling Russell brothers didn't realise they were describing a new species and assumed it was a European hamster. The first to identify the golden hamster as a separate species was George Waterhouse of the London Zoological Society. In 1839 he identified a female whose preserved remains are apparently (according to the British Hamster Association) still kicking around somewhere in London's Natural History Museum.

However, any sustained attempts to breed captured golden hamsters had died out before 1930, when Israel Aharoni, a zoologist working in Jerusalem, went out looking for hamsters on behalf of his colleague Saul Adler (who evidently had something better to do). Aharoni hunted down a female golden hamster and her litter of eleven puppies with the help of some locals, again in Aleppo. Joy quickly turned to tragedy as the mother bit the head off one of her own children and was then dunked in cyanide by a villager. All in a day's work for hamster-rustlers. However, some of the litter were successfully bred, and eventually made the leap from laboratory animals to household pets after being imported into England; and it is indeed the case that all the *pet* golden hamsters in the world derive from Aharoni's find – hence their alternative name of Syrian hamsters.

However, while extremely rare, golden hamsters do still exist in the wild in Syria and Israel, and have been captured and bred in the laboratory since Aharoni's time.

VERDICT: FALSE, BUT ONLY JUST

Hamsters might seem lazy, but that's because they're nocturnal fitness fanatics – they can run between 5 and 10 kilometres (between 3 and 6 miles) in a night without getting bored of the same wheel.

If you drop a tarantula, it will shatter

YOU'D HAVE TO BE PRETTY BRAVE to pick up a tarantula to start with, although contrary to popular belief, the tarantula's bite is not fatal to humans. It can be pretty painful, however – and if you're especially unlucky, that may be the moment when you discover you're allergic to tarantula venom, resulting in anaphylactic shock. Some species also have 'urticating hairs', which are barbed abdominal hairs that can be fired in the direction of an attacker. If you've got any sense, then, don't go round provoking tarantulas by calling them 'monkey spiders' or offering to 'settle it outside' (it's not worth it).

In general, picking up tarantulas is not advised at all: if you really want to have one crawl up your arm, you should allow it to crawl onto your hand first, but not pick it up. This is because, although they might look quite soft and furry, tarantulas have very fragile exoskeletons. A fall from even a few centimetres seriously risks shattering the exoskeleton, or simply rupturing the abdomen; either way, it's likely to be fatal.

Tarantulas shed their exoskeletons on a regular basis, something they usually do on their backs. Which means that if you just happen to come across an upside-down tarantula, it's neither dead nor breakdancing, but is in a particularly vulnerable condition and shouldn't be touched.

So, don't touch them while they're moulting, don't pick them up, don't drop them, don't provoke them, don't get in the way of their javelin hairs. *Just get a cat instead, you attention-seeking 'look at me with my extreme pet' moron.*

VERDICT: TRUE

During the filming of *Raiders of the Lost Ark*, although the 4,000 'snake extras' made it through unharmed, a tarantula was accidentally dropped and killed on set, presumably shattering on a roll of gaffer tape or a technician's foot.

Dogs' legs are getting shorter

YOU CAN MAKE THIS CLAIM as confidently as you like, as long as no one asks you what you actually mean. Or if you have any evidence for it. Does it mean that during any single dog's lifetime, its legs get shorter – perhaps due to the weight of the dog's body bearing down on the limbs over the years? Or does it mean that over successive generations, the average length of a dog's leg has decreased?

The second option seems the more probable suggestion. But if you're losing sleep about the idea that a few years from now we'll be seeing massive Great Danes with tiny sausage-legs, you'd be better off worrying about that colony of mutant alligators breeding in the sewers beneath your house.

In archaeological contexts, decreased leg lengths in canine skeletons can suggest a process of domestication from wolf to dog – suggesting that dogs' legs have become shorter as they have adapted to living with humans – but it is not a foolproof

indication unless accompanied by
other factors such as the location of
the skeleton relative to human
activity.

The smaller the dog, the smaller
the ratio between the length of its
leg and its overall height; so dogs'
legs get shorter as dogs get shorter.
But in general, the problem is that
there are so many different dog
breeds, with huge variation in
leg length, that there is no overall sense of dogs' legs getting
shorter or longer over time. When
it comes to breed popularity, owners
are as fickle as fashion-magazine editors. Next week, for example,
Rod Stewart could be photographed out on the town with a 'leggy
hound', and everyone might hastily start breeding for this trait, in
order to meet the huge surge in demand for spindly legged dogs.

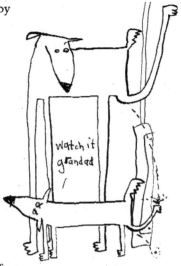

VERDICT: WHO KNOWS, AND WHO CARES?

Policemen are getting younger.

SHOWBIZ

Mel Blanc was allergic to carrots

IF YOU DON'T KNOW WHO Mel Blanc was, you might be thinking: 'So what?' However, if you know that he provided the voice for the carrot-munching Bugs Bunny, it may seem slightly more significant.

Blanc voiced so many cartoon characters – Daffy Duck, Sylvester the Cat and Barney Rubble, to name just a few – that it wouldn't be entirely surprising to find that he had a contrary reaction to one of the Toons' regular pastimes. After all, he probably didn't particularly enjoy being hunted by a shotgun-wielding fathead, chasing canaries or using his bare feet to power an ancient forerunner of the motor car.

Nevertheless, the 'carrot allergy' claim has stuck because he had to crunch carrots during recording. It's been suggested that on occasion the allergy made his vocal cords swell up painfully, and that he would save any 'carrot scenes' until the end of each recording session, leaving them to be edited into the main dialogue afterwards.

Clearly this story has proved enduring. However, Blanc

described the real problem in his 1988 autobiography, stating that he found it 'impossible to chew, swallow, and be ready to say my next line'. He added that the production team would 'stop recording so that I could spit out the carrot into a wastebasket and then proceed with the script'. He certainly said that he didn't 'especially' like carrots, 'at least not raw' – but that's a far cry from an allergy. If you go to the doctor claiming to be allergic to carrots because you don't 'especially' like them, but they're all right cooked, you'll receive pretty short shrift.

VERDICT: THAT'S ALL NONSENSE!

An avid collector of antique timepieces, Mel Blanc owned the first watch ever made, from 1510.

Bob Holness played the saxophone on Gerry Rafferty's 'Baker Street'

JUST ABOUT EVERY PERSON in Britain must have recounted or been astonished by the suggestion that a TV quiz show host could be behind the 1978 hit's famous saxophone riff. Unusually for an urban myth, the origins of this totally unfounded claim can be pinpointed to one man: music journalist Stuart Maconie.

The writer 'fessed up in his 2004 memoir *Cider With Roadies*, explaining that while writing for the *NME*, he started inventing 'trivia' for the 'Thrills' column, as a parody of the sort of ill-researched nonsense perpetually repeated in newspapers about how the Great Wall of China is visible from space (see p. 279 of this book if you're interested).

In fact, the classic saxophone part on 'Baker Street' was played by Raphael Ravenscroft, an accomplished session musician and the author of *The Complete Saxophone Player*. A slightly more plausible 'fact' is that the part was originally written for guitar, with only a short saxophone section intended for the song's introduction; but Ravenscroft took up the main riff because the guitar player was running late.

Bob Holness, meanwhile, appeared on the radio throughout the 1970s and was a presenter on London's LBC when 'Baker Street' was released. He had not yet risen to national fame with *Blockbusters*.

VERDICT: FICTITIOUS

Interestingly, the second run of the US version of *Blockbusters* was hosted by Bill Rafferty, so perhaps this was the inspiration – conscious or otherwise – for Stuart Maconie's fabrication.

ZZ Top are named after a brand of toilet paper

THE LEGENDARY ZZ Top evolved from The Moving Sidewalks and The American Blues to become, in 1970, the blues-rock power trio we know (and love?) today. 'That Little Ol' Band From Texas' became global music icons in the 1980s, yet despite all that's been written about them, the origins of the band's name remain as elusive as the chances of their drummer growing a beard.

Theories advanced to date – some deliberately propagated by the band to tantalise their fans – range from the boring (guitarist Billy Gibbons saw the letters 'ZZ' and 'Top' next to each other) and the very boring (Billy saw some Z-shaped braces supporting a pair of

barn doors), to the vaguely plausible (Billy was a fan of Texan blues singer Arzell 'Z.Z.' Hill) and the secretive (in many interviews the band simply refuse to discuss it).

In Billy's book *Rock + Roll Gearhead*, which tells his life story 'through his amazing collection of custom automobiles and guitars', he claims to have noticed two handbills in his apartment, one advertising Z.Z. Hill and the other B.B. King. Combining them as Z.Z. King still sounded too much like B.B. King, but then he decided that '*King* is like the *Top*'. This is not necessarily any more truthful (or any more comprehensible) than the other suggestions.

One of the more believable provenances is that the name was inspired by not one but *two* brands of rolling paper: Zig-Zag and Top. Yes, *rolling paper* – for rolling your own cigarettes – not *toilet roll*. The confusion perhaps arose outside the USA, where Zig-Zag and Top may not be so well known.

VERDICT: NO SUCH TOILET PAPER

Anyone who believes that toilet roll would be marketed with the abrasive-sounding 'Zig-Zag' brand name must be potty.

Marilyn Monroe had six toes

LET'S GET THE PEDANTIC BIT out of the way first: yes, yes, most people have six toes, because most people have ten in total. In Marilyn Monroe's case, however, it has long been alleged that she had eleven toes in total, due to a 'spare toe' on her left foot. Like the facts about 'Baker Street' (see p. 58) and Claude Monet (see p. 213), the six-toes story can be blamed on one person. But rather than the result of humorous invention or mistaken identity, this claim may have been motivated by publicity-seeking.

In 1991 Joseph Jasgur and Jeannie Sakol published *The Birth of Marilyn*, a book of previously unseen photographs. Two of the pictures, taken just before she signed with Twentieth Century Fox, do seem to show six toes on her left foot. But there are many other pictures (some in the same book, taken just a few days later) that quite clearly show only five toes. And there is no medical or anecdotal evidence that Marilyn Monroe ever had six toes on her left foot.

Despite this, and despite not noticing her extra toe during the actual shoot in 1946, Joseph Jasgur claimed in his 1991 book that the photographs *proved* she had eleven toes. So, either she was born with ten toes, grew an extra one that the photographer didn't notice, and which then disappeared within a couple of days leaving no discernible mark – or the 'sixth toe' is a bit of sand and a trick of the light, and Joseph Jasgur wanted to drum up lots of publicity for his book.

VERDICT: TOE-TALLY UNTRUE

Despite having been dead for nearly half a century, Marilyn

Monroe somehow manages to have an official website at
www.marilynmonroe.com, which tells us that she was 1947's Miss
California Artichoke Queen.

Elvis Costello's dad was the secret lemonade drinker

THIS ISN'T SOME EUPHEMISTIC WAY of accusing Elvis
Costello's dad of having a heroin addiction, but a reference to the
classic television adverts for R. White's Lemonade, which were
first screened in the UK in 1973 and appeared regularly
throughout the following decade.

The commercials are memorable for the bespectacled, pyjama-
wearing man who sneaks downstairs in the middle of the night
to raid the fridge for lemonade – only to be caught by his wife.
Mid-sneak, he mimes to a song about being a secret lemonade
drinker, sung in a wavering voice not dissimilar to that of the
'other' Elvis. The guy in the pyjamas was *not* Elvis Costello's dad,
but the actor Julian Chagrin, who was later nominated for two
Oscars (for producing short films, rather than miming on adverts
in his jim-jams).

In addition to the fridge-raiding storyline, there were two
related adverts known as 'Phone Box' and 'Pop Singer'. The latter
(which was in fact the original advert but is not as fondly remembered) did indeed feature Elvis Costello's dad, Ross MacManus,
performing the 'Secret Lemonade Drinker' song – which was written by him and used in all the adverts. Appearing as a backing
vocalist in the 'Pop Singer' version was his son Declan, who later

combined Presley's first name with his grandmother's maiden name to become Elvis Costello.

Other famous names to have appeared in R. White's adverts over the years include Ronnie Corbett, John McEnroe and John 'Headbutts' Otway.

VERDICT: MORE OR LESS

In 1996, British rock group Mansun released a song that, for legal reasons, had the inverted title of 'Lemonade Secret Drinker'; it portrayed a rather less genial outlook on life.

That dweeby kid out of *The Wonder Years* grew up to become Marilyn Manson

THIS IS A CLASSIC URBAN MYTH that has, disappointingly, no basis in fact. But it makes for a captivating story: the transformation from an introverted teenage geek in a warm and nostalgic view of 1960s America, to a controversial 'shock rocker', the thorn in the side of conservative parents everywhere.

Many who espouse this claim almost seem to believe that the character in question (Kevin Arnold's friend Paul Pfeiffer) is somehow a real person rather than a fictional creation. The part was played by Josh Saviano, a child actor who in reality left show business to study at Yale and then work for a law firm, and he is apparently amused by the constant allegations of his conversion to the dark side.

Marilyn Manson, meanwhile, started out life as Brian Warner, and is seven years older than Josh Saviano. When *The Wonder Years* first screened in 1988 the nineteen-year-old Brian was taking a journalism course at Broward Community College in Florida. After interviewing bands for the college newspaper and local magazines, he decided he wanted to perform, so he formed a group that eventually morphed into the Marilyn Manson who outraged America in the 1990s.

VERDICT: COMPLETELY MADE-UP

In his spare time, Marilyn Manson paints watercolours, and in 2002 he managed to flog one called *Harlequin Jack and the Absinthe Bunny* to Ozzy Osbourne's son Jack.

Willy Wonka and the Chocolate Factory was financed by the Quaker Oats Company

THE 1971 FILM OF Roald Dahl's classic children's book – not to be confused with Tim Burton's 2005 version, which restored the original title of *Charlie and the Chocolate Factory* – was not a hit on first release. Over the years, however, it gradually acquired a cult following, boosted by repeated inclusion in Christmas TV schedules and, later, VHS and DVD sales. So has that friendly-looking white-haired guy with the hat been raking it in all these years? Well, not quite.

In the early 1970s it seems the Quaker Oats Company could afford to think big. Not long after buying out toy manufacturer Fisher-Price (which they sold off in 1991), they were looking to promote a new chocolate bar, and were persuaded by producer David L. Wolper to do a movie tie-in, by financing the film to the tune of $2.9 million and calling their new product the Wonka bar.

Although the author drafted the first screenplay, director Mel Stuart brought in David Seltzer (later of *The Omen* fame) to rework the script – with the end result being roundly hated by Roald Dahl. By the time the film was released, Quaker Oats had shelved the Wonka bar idea.

Distributors Paramount let the film go after their seven-year deal expired, whereupon Quaker Oats realised they knew more about cereals than movies, so they sold the rights to Warner Bros. for $500,000. By the 1990s – when the Wonka bar finally resurfaced, manufactured by Nestlé – Quaker Oats were probably choking on their porridge as they saw how well everything was going.

VERDICT: TRUE

Roald Dahl constructed an exact replica of Dylan Thomas's writing hut at the bottom of his garden; off-limits to everyone except himself, it was never cleaned during his lifetime.

The Girl from Ipanema is now an MP

THIS IS A CHARMING BLEND of a song with real life: the idea being that the subject of the 1960s hit 'The Girl from Ipanema' was a real person and grew up to represent her constituency as a member of parliament.

The girl who inspired the song can certainly be identified as Heloísa ('Helô') Pinheiro, née Pinto, who was around eighteen years old when 'Garota de Ipanema' was written in 1962. Vinícius de Moraes, who wrote the original Portuguese lyrics, and Antonio ('Tom') Jobim, who wrote the music, used to frequent a bar in the Ipanema beach area of Rio de Janeiro. The two middle-aged songwriters would sit there every day – at least ordering a drink for the sake of appearances, one hopes – and stare at Helô as she walked past (does anyone else find that a bit weird?). Helô wasn't generally in the habit of staring back, although they must have got talking at some point since Tom Jobim was best man at her wedding in 1966.

Although something of a celebrity as a result of the song's global success, particularly after the 'tall and tan and young and lovely' English lyrics were written by Norman Gimbel, Helô Pinheiro has not, so far, made it into politics. She has, however, twice made it into the pages of *Playboy* magazine, most recently in 2003 when she appeared in a photoshoot together with her daughter (does anyone else find that a bit weird?).

In 2001 the late songwriters' relatives sued Helô Pinheiro for opening a shop named after the song, claiming that she was somehow unfairly cashing in. The miserable gits.

VERDICT: NOT TRUE
Yet.

There's a child's ghost in *Three Men and a Baby*

A CHILD'S GHOST? In a film? What? Well, the theory goes that in a scene where Ted Danson's character and his mother are walking through his shared apartment, a ghost is visible through the curtains. More specifically, the ghost is supposed to be that of a boy who died in the house – as a result of suicide or murder, depending who is spouting this nonsense – where the scene was filmed.

Since all of *Three Men and a Baby*'s interior scenes were shot in a studio, the 'died in the house' angle is clearly false – as if it was ever likely to be true. As for the ghost itself, it's a smaller-than-life cardboard cut-out of Ted Danson in a dinner jacket, which was intended to be used in a sub-plot that never made it into the final film. The cut-out – or a similar one, at any rate – is more clearly visible in a later scene.

Maybe you're thinking: '*Surely* no one would actually believe this.' But just ask actress Jemima Rooper, who confessed in British newspaper *Metro* to having been terrified when watching the scene with her best friend: 'We both saw this little boy and we freaked. We gave these blood-curdling screams, my friend started crying, I phoned my mum.' These reactions would have been understandable if they'd been watching *Jack*, but *Three Men and a Baby*? Extraordinary. Admittedly, though, this was in the context of trying to hawk her latest TV series, which happened to have a supernatural theme.

VERDICT: RUBBISH

Three Men and a Baby, directed by Mr Spock out of *Star Trek*, was a remake of the 1985 French film *Trois hommes et un couffin*, which definitely does not feature any ghosts.

Mike Nesmith of The Monkees is the heir to the Tipp-Ex fortune

IN 1951, SO THE STORY GOES, Bette Graham was working as a secretary in her home town of Dallas, Texas. She wanted to be a full-time artist, but she had recently divorced and had a young son to raise. Frustrated in her day job at having to re-type whole pages whenever she made an error, she tried to apply a principle she had learned as an artist – to paint over a mistake with a corrected version – by taking her white tempera paint and a brush to work.

Word quickly spread in office circles and she improved the formula to the point where, in 1956, it was marketed commercially as Mistake Out. That was a duff name, so she later changed it to Liquid Paper (and presumably painted out the old company name rather than getting all her stationery reprinted). By the time it had become a multimillion-dollar business in the 1970s, her son Mike, who retained his father's surname Nesmith, had become famous as one quarter of The Monkees and was already moving on to solo projects.

Tipp-Ex, on the other hand, was invented in Germany by Otto Carls, initially as a correction paper in 1959 and only in 1965 as a fluid. The fact that in Europe Tipp-Ex has become as synonymous with correction fluid as Liquid Paper has in North America probably explains why Mike Nesmith's mum is often credited with inventing Tipp-Ex. Then again, in the States there's also Wite-Out (invented by George Kloosterhouse and Edwin Johanknecht in 1966), and in New Zealand there's, er, Twink – which could have disastrous consequences if marketed elsewhere.

VERDICT: CORRECTION REQUIRED

Bette Graham sold off Liquid Paper shortly before her death in 1980; so while Mike did inherit a tidy sum from his mother's estate, he didn't inherit the company.

Fay Wray was a partial vegetarian

WHAT CAN THIS *possibly* mean? Fay Wray played the heroine Ann Darrow in the original 1933 film of *King Kong*, that much is clear – but how could she be a 'partial' vegetarian? If it's supposed to mean 'eating mostly vegetarian food but not all the time', isn't that the same as just *not* being a vegetarian? It's a bit like saying you're a partial teetotaller because you only go out boozing at the weekend.

This is the sort of 'fact' that, having been written once, is then copied and pasted into every obituary on the planet. It is usually uttered in the same breath as the claim that Fay Wray 'always tried to stick to her rule of not eating late at night', or that she 'was still driving a car well into her nineties'. Hardly the most astonishing of revelations about an actress who

appeared in around 100 films and performed on stage opposite Cary Grant.

Still, since you can't libel the dead (see p. 177) here are some more controversial, sue-if-you-dare facts about Fay Wray: she suffered from mild seasickness; she disliked dogs; and she once invented a blue-cheese soda. Actually, she also believed in reincarnation, so if she was right about that, libel laws may need to be hastily re-drafted.

Ironically, as a giant gorilla, Kong himself could have claimed to be a 'partial' vegetarian, since a gorilla's diet is plant-based except for a tiny amount of insects. However, Fay Wray is not known to have deliberately eaten insects.

VERDICT: MEANINGLESS

While remaking *King Kong*, lardy director Peter Jackson stopped eating meat for health reasons, and subsequently became a *total* vegetarian – take that, Fay Wray, you early-night-dining, blue-cheese-drinking dog-disliker!

Jack Lemmon was born in a lift

THIS MERITS COMPULSORY inclusion in any conversation about the star of classics such as *The Odd Couple*, *Some Like It Hot* and *Glengarry Glen Ross*. Somehow the late actor's legendary comic timing and acclaimed character portrayals pale into insignificance compared to the issue of how – or rather, where – he arrived in the world. It's possible that pub-fact fans remember Billy Wilder's classic comedy *The Apartment*, where C.C. Baxter (Lemmon) falls in love with the elevator-girl Fran Kubelik (Shirley MacLaine), and can't believe that this coincides, vaguely, with his own personal beginnings.

Lemmon was indeed born in the elevator of an apartment building on 8 February 1925, in Newton, Massachusetts. His heavily pregnant mother was involved in a particularly thrilling game of bridge, and refused to leave the table in time to make it to the hospital.

It is not known what floor the elevator had reached at the moment of Jack's delivery, or whether Mrs Lemmon won the game.

VERDICT: TRUE

Interestingly, an inaccurate retelling of this event is thought to have inspired Aerosmith's 1989 hit 'Love in an Elevator'.

Frank Beard is the only member of ZZ Top who doesn't have a beard

IT DOES SEEM TOO ABSURD to be coincidence that of the three members of veteran Texas blues-rockers ZZ Top, the only one who doesn't sport a massive, floor-sweeping beard should be called Frank Beard. At the very least, you'd expect to find out that the drummer was born Francis Smith and adopted the name for comedy purposes.

But no: it's his real surname, and indeed the other two band members (guitarist Billy Gibbons and bassist Dusty Hill) acquired their 'trademark facial hair' only after being in the band with him for six or seven years. More astonishing still is the fact that Dusty and Billy independently decided to cultivate extensive beards during a three-year career break in the late 1970s. They discovered that, as Billy put it, 'lazy and not shaving make a fine combination'.

There's no doubt that the beards in question – along with trench coats, sunglasses and leggy blondes – helped raise the band to the level of superstars in the early days of MTV, and by 1984 each beard was valued at a million dollars by Gillette, who unsuccessfully attempted to persuade Dusty and Billy to shave them off for a TV advert.

Frank Beard may not cultivate a beard because he's too busy playing with his 'remote-control hot tub', which, according to numerous ZZ Top fan websites, can be 'started from his limo on the way up the drive'. The origins and validity of this claim are unclear, but one hopes that Frank is always able to get straight from the limo into a heated tub without wasting a moment of his precious time.

VERDICT: TRUE
Frank does, however, tend to sport a small moustache.

New Order are fascists

'MANCHESTER'S FINEST BAND', according to New Order, must be tired of being accused of fascist tendencies. Mind you, if they actually *were* fascists, then presumably such accusations would constitute generous praise rather than stark criticism.

Still, they brought it on themselves. They started out in a punk vein as Stiff Kittens (suggested by the Buzzcocks) and then as Warsaw (inspired by David Bowie's song 'Warszawa'). However, because another punk band was doing the rounds as Warsaw Pakt, they needed a new name and apparently chose the most controversial one they could think of: Joy Division, the term used for concentration camp brothels in the 1955 novel *The House of Dolls* by Ka-Tzetnik 135633 (pen-name of Auschwitz survivor Yehiel De-Nur). They also recited from the book in a 1977 recording of their song 'No Love Lost'. Shouting 'You all forgot Rudolf Hess!' at the start of a live version of 'At a Later Date' and designing a Hitler Youth-style cover for *An Ideal for Living* didn't help.

After Ian Curtis died, the band re-established themselves under the equally controversial name of New Order, which evoked Hitler's *'neue Ordnung'* – the way he'd like to have seen Europe end up – though they later said this derived from a newspaper article about the Khmer Rouge's proposed 'new order' for Cambodia.

Despite decades of accusations, New Order have repeatedly denied having any political sympathies with Hitler or fascism in general. The Nazi symbolism – similarly used by Siouxsie Sioux, the Sex Pistols, Damon Hill (see p. 85) and others – was designed to court controversy, and everyone involved now apologetically reflects on how they misunderstood its effects.

VERDICT: FALSE

The short-lived Warsaw Pakt recorded, pressed, packaged and released their only album, *Needle Time*, between 10 p.m. on a Saturday night and 7 p.m. the following evening.

Bob Holness was the first person to play James Bond

POOR BOB HOLNESS: for some reason the *Blockbusters* host seems to be the subject of every rumour under the sun. One minute he's being accused of playing the sax (see p. 58), and the next minute  someone will try to tell you he wrote the 'Secret Lemonade Drinker' music – which was actually written by Elvis Costello's dad (see p. 62). Perhaps this business about James Bond is just another myth, invented so that people can joke about 007 saying 'Can I have a P please, Q,' or Auric Goldfinger cackling 'No, Mr Bond, I expect you to put yourself on the Hot Spot!'

'First person' depends on which entertainment medium you are talking about. Sean Connery was certainly the first actor to portray James Bond in the movies, starting with *Dr. No* in 1962. But Bob Holness had already played the part on radio, in a 1956 adaptation of *Moonraker* in South Africa. Nevertheless, Bob Holness himself was still not the first overall: in 1954 CBS produced a TV version of *Casino Royale* starring the prolific actor Barry Nelson.

Casino Royale was Ian Fleming's first Bond novel. In the CBS version, 'Jimmy' Bond was American rather than British, but it was otherwise fairly faithful to the book – unlike the 1967 film spoof *Casino Royale*, in which numerous actors and actresses passed themselves off as James Bond, Jimmy Bond or 007 (David Niven, Peter Sellers, Woody Allen, Terence Cooper, Ursula Andress and Daliah Lavi). A rather more straight-faced adaptation of *Casino Royale* was chosen to be the twenty-first official Bond movie, with Daniel Craig in the lead role.

VERDICT: FALSE

Bob Holness's career has received a massive boost in recent years due to the touch-screen version of *Blockbusters* featured on numerous pub quiz machines.

The Beatles wrote the song 'Dear Prudence' for Mia Farrow's sister

IN EARLY 1968 Prudence Farrow and her more famous sister Mia (who by that time had already married and divorced Frank Sinatra) visited an ashram in India run by the Maharishi Mahesh Yogi, credited with introducing transcendental meditation to Western culture. The retreat at Rishikesh was also attended by the Beatles, Donovan and Mike Love of The Beach Boys.

It was a very creative period for the group formerly trading as the Fab Four, who were said to have written over 40 songs during their stay, many of which appeared on the 'White Album' later that year. 'Dear Prudence' – primarily a John Lennon composition – was written as a musical means to entice Prudence Farrow to come out of her room, where she was apparently spending too much time meditating on her own. In using Prudence's rather unusual name Lennon probably also intended a more general interpretation of the song, as a call to overly cautious people to come out and see what the world has to offer.

Another song on the 'White Album' in which Lennon specifically describes his experiences of India is 'Sexy Sadie'. He had the title 'Maharishi' in mind, but later changed it for legal reasons – and cleaned up the foul-mouthed lyrics that expressed in no uncertain terms his disillusionment in the Maharishi. One reason cited for the Beatles' collective disappointment was the allegation that the supposedly celibate Maharishi had made a pass at Mia Farrow. Another version of events relates that the Maharishi ordered the Beatles to leave because of their drug-taking and general time-wasting.

VERDICT: TRUE

The Maharishi Mahesh Yogi has always denied trying it on with Mia Farrow, and has certainly never been convicted of being a seedy con-man.

Trevor McDonald taught himself English by reading a dictionary

It would take a pretty long time, wouldn't it? Let's suppose that French was the official language of Trinidad, birthplace of veteran newsreader Sir Trevor. So, if his first language was French, he must have read an entire French–English dictionary. No matter how unputdownable a dictionary may be and no matter how much time you have on your hands (bear in mind that in the *Collins Robert French Dictionary* the entry for '*à*' is a page and a half long), simply reading it all the way through is not going to give you a thorough grasp of English grammar, pronunciation and vocabulary.

French *isn't* the official language of Trinidad anyway – it's English, which was Trevor McDonald's first language. And no, he didn't somehow learn his first language from a monolingual dictionary; he learned it in the normal way. However, he has said that when growing up, he *refined* his English by listening to the BBC World Service, taking elocution lessons, participating in public-speaking contests and, indeed, reading a large number of books, including the dictionary. The overblown claim that he *taught himself English* by reading the dictionary may stem from a comment made by Lionel Dixon, a former colleague at Radio Trinidad, who told the *Guardian* newspaper in 1995: 'He lived with a dictionary. He *was* the Oxford dictionary.'

Knighted in 1999, Sir Trevor is now viewed as an elder statesman of broadcasting, whose excellent command of English has been recognised in public polls and through his appointment as the head of a government panel to promote the use of 'better English' – a job what he is said to of done proper good at.

VERDICT: MASSIVELY EXAGGERATED

Trevor McDonald was christened George McDonald, because his father forgot to call him Trevor.

Phil Collins wrote 'In the Air Tonight' following an incident in which he witnessed a man drowning but was too far away to do anything about it

THIS IS MORE OF A straightforward urban myth than a pub fact, but to this day people still claim it to be the origin of the song. There are numerous variations on the theme, many suggesting that Collins saw someone else failing to help a drowning man; and others claim that Collins invited the non-helping witness to attend the concert where he premiered the song, so that he could shine an accusatory spotlight on the guilty party during the performance.

There is no truth in any of the claims, which probably owe their origins to a confused reading of Collins's anger: 'if you told me you were drowning, I would not lend a hand' – because 'I was there and I saw what you did'. That's a big 'if'. The lyrics do not, metaphorically or otherwise, describe anyone drowning.

Although this rumour surfaced within a couple of years of the song's first release in 1981, the Internet boosted its momentum massively during the 1990s, and by 2000 the myth was to feature in Eminem's hit 'Stan' (in which the song is referred to, bafflingly, as 'In the Air of the Night'). Interestingly, however, on the radio edit of 'Stan', not only is there no swearing or muffled screaming – there is no mention of Phil Collins. Could it be that censors (or those in fear of the censors) regard mention of Phil Collins as every bit as corrupting on youthful ears as a barrage of four-letter words and violence against women?

VERDICT: SUNK

Collins has wearily tried to point out that the song was written during his divorce from his first wife, and that it isn't about any specific incident, just 'the bitter side of a separation'.

The London Astoria used to be a Branston Pickle factory

THE CHARING CROSS ROAD VENUE has changed ownership and function a number of times during its history. Its current incarnation as one of London's biggest live-music venues began in 1986 following a decade as a theatre; and previously all or part of the site had been used as (variously) a cinema, a 'gentleman's variety club', a ballroom and a music hall.

The present building opened in 1927 as a cinema and ballroom, constructed on the site of a factory owned by Crosse & Blackwell, who had offices in Soho Square backing onto it. The company first had offices built at 18 Soho Square, and expanded into numbers 20 and 21 during the second half of the nineteenth century, before demolishing and rebuilding number 20 in 1924. Another factory was situated not far away, in King Street, Covent Garden.

Crosse & Blackwell first started making Branston Pickle in 1922, shortly before the Charing Cross Road factory closed – and as indicated by the name, it was actually produced in the Staffordshire village of Branston. So while the Soho factory did make pickles (as well as jam and other preserves), it did not manufacture Branston Pickle specifically. According to Ben

Weinreb and Christopher Hibbert's *The London Encyclopaedia*, during its time as a cinema the building was known informally as 'the Jam Factory' because of its origins (not because the walls and floors of the ageing interior were as sticky as they are today).

Despite the Astoria's popularity, the site is currently facing demolition to make way for a ticketing hall within the new Tottenham Court Road Crossrail station.

VERDICT: ALMOST TRUE!

In 2004 a fire gutted the 'actual' Branston Pickle factory in Bury St Edmunds (where production had been relocated after the brand was bought by Premier Foods), temporarily causing a massive cheddar–pickle imbalance throughout the UK and resulting in extensive psychological trauma for ploughman's lunch addicts, who were forced to eat pickleless cold turkey.

'Get Back' was originally a racist diatribe demanding that immigrants should 'get back to where they once belonged'

FOR A LONG TIME 'Get Back' simply represented a barn-storming end to the Beatles' career, coming at the end of the *Let It Be* album, which was released around the time of their official break-up. The song was made particularly memorable by the Beatles' 1969 performance on the roof of the Apple building at 3 Savile Row, London, and was noted for the live feel of the album version, free of the saccharine 'Wall of Sound' production that Phil Spector decided to add elsewhere. (Neither the album nor the single versions were actually from one live take, but that's another story.)

Gradually, though, tales of 'racist' bootleg versions of the song surfaced, with the implication that Paul had originally written an extremist rant that the rest of the group had to tone down.

The genesis of the song actually appears to fuse two ideas: a desire to parody the attitudes towards immigration embodied in Enoch Powell's recent 'Rivers of Blood' speech; and inspiration from the line 'get back to where you should be' in George's song 'Sour Milk Sea' (recorded with little success by Jackie Lomax). The two most controversial bootlegs (known to Beatle buffs as 'The Commonwealth Song' and 'No Pakistanis') feature lines such as 'immigrants had better go home' and 'don't dig no Pakistanis taking all the people's jobs', and Paul and John generally banging on about the Commonwealth. However, aside from the fact that 'The Commonwealth Song' clearly mentions Enoch Powell in a satirical manner, studio out-takes record Paul's explanations that it was a protest song.

VERDICT: TRUE ... BUT SATIRICAL

Meanwhile, John was allegedly convinced that the underlying message of 'Get Back' was Paul having a go at Yoko.

Norman Wisdom is massive in Albania

THE ENGLISH COMIC may be an institution in the UK (and in the Isle of Man, his adopted home), but in Albania Norman Wisdom's popularity is in another league altogether. The veteran entertainer is fêted as a folk hero for his portrayal of the hapless underdog variously called Norman Pitkin, Norman Hackett, Norman Truscott, Norman Puckle, Norman Shields or just plain Norman in numerous film comedies of the 1950s and 1960s.

When a charity visit to Albania in 2001 coincided with the appearance of the England football squad, chanting crowds in the capital city of Tirana made it clear that Wisdom was a bigger celebrity than David Beckham. And in 2002, as documented in the book *One Hit Wonderland* by Tony Hawks (the comedian, *not* the skateboarder Tony 'Birdman' Hawk), Sir Norman had a hit single in the Albanian charts. When he announced his intention to retire after his ninetieth birthday – he could be forgiven for wanting to take it easy at that age – Albania practically went into a state of national mourning.

So why Albania? It's all because of the Communist dictator Enver Hoxha, who decided that under his regime the only Western films that were permitted were those of 'Pitkini', as Norman Wisdom is known there. The bizarre reasoning was that Pitkini's slapstick antics represented not just good clean fun but the struggles of the proletariat against the capitalist masters. Sadly perhaps, Sir Norman's popularity in Albania is likely to decline over the coming years, now that younger generations are not force-fed a cultural diet of a guy in a flat cap shouting 'Mr Grimsdale!' in a high-pitched voice.

VERDICT: TRUE

When he was thirteen, Norman Wisdom walked from London to Cardiff to get a job working on a cargo ship.

If you dial 1 on a phone, it will connect you to the Queen; however, she is extremely busy and will have you imprisoned if you phone her up without good reason

CLEARLY, NO ADULT would believe this, but it is something often told to small children. Why? Surely, upon hearing about this forbidden telephonic fruit, they will either be thoroughly frustrated and even more tantrum-prone than usual or, if they are rather sceptical or foolhardy, be tempted into risking a call (and hence imprisonment). As with many things parents tell their children, it's probably a case of keeping them occupied while they're locked in the car eating crisps and their parents are having a good time in the pub.

A variant of this scare story is that dialling 0 will connect you to the operator – a single person who busily deals with all the operator calls in the world; so if you waste the operator's time, she'll recognise you next time you phone. Those with particularly malicious elder siblings may even have believed that the operator would have to leave a hospital operating theatre to take your call or perhaps speak to you while performing surgery, so it had better be important because a life might be at stake.

A curious child might start to consider what the Queen would regard as a 'good reason' for calling. Being locked in a car, perhaps. Disappointingly, however, on many mobile phones dialling 1 will simply connect to voicemail.

VERDICT: DARERS GO FIRST

Kids, don't believe the hype: dialling 1 or 0 from a landline does nothing – but it is charged at £40 per minute so your parents will get very angry when they find out.

The Jacksons' song 'Blame It on the Boogie' was written by a completely different Michael Jackson

THE DISCO CLASSIC 'Blame It on the Boogie' was released by The Jacksons as a single in 1978 and was the first track on their *Destiny* album. At this stage, the group had mutated from The Jackson Family and The Jackson 5 to become The Jacksons, with the core line-up consisting of Michael, Jackie, Tito, Marlon and Randy (who had replaced Jermaine). For the first time, the brothers produced their own album and, according to the liner notes, wrote all their own material. Or rather, they claimed that all the songs were 'written by The Jacksons', which was technically true.

Individually, each of *Destiny*'s eight songs was written by Michael on his own, or Michael and Randy, or the whole group – except for 'Blame It on the Boogie', which was actually written by

Michael 'Mick' Jackson. It's pure coincidence that Mick Jackson's song ended up on an album by The Jacksons. The British soul and disco artist had in fact written it with Dave Jackson (his brother) and Elmar Krohn, who had previously played together with Mick's other brother Pete in a band called, would you believe it, Jacko. In a further twist of improbability, in 1977 Mick had released his first solo single, 'You Turn Me On' – which his record company mistakenly credited to the name of Nick Jackson.

Mick had hoped that 'Boogie' would be recorded by Stevie Wonder, but it was picked up by The Jacksons' management as a sure-fire banker. As expected, it was a hit – for both The Jacksons *and* Mick Jackson, whose own recording was released within days of the cover version. At the time the stand-off was hailed as 'The Battle of the Boogie', with The Jacksons' version charting slightly higher than Mick's on both sides of the Atlantic.

VERDICT: TRUE

Mick Jackson is also not related to British beer connoisseur Michael 'The Beer Hunter' Jackson.

There's a Def Leppard guitar solo by Damon Hill

IN THE MID-1990S DAMON HILL took over the mantle of 'the only English Formula One driver that non-racing fans have heard of' from Nigel Mansell: a coveted one-in, one-out media position presently occupied by Jensen Button, and once inhabited by Damon's own father Graham.

Before he rose to fame and became the 1996 Formula One World

Champion, Damon was in a school punk band called Sex, Hitler and the Hormones, but it was not until he retired from racing that he set up his own official group, Damon and the Conrods (although they seem to have mysteriously vanished). Meanwhile, in 1999 he got talking to Def Leppard's lead singer Joe Elliott at a number of showbiz parties – and ended up playing the ten-second guitar solo on 'Demolition Man', the opening track on the band's comeback album *Euphoria*.

In addition to Def Leppard and one-off performances with other racers like Johnny Herbert and Eddie Jordan, Damon has also played guitar with George Harrison, Eric Clapton and the SAS Band (an ever-changing all-star band run by Spike Edney, who played keyboards with Queen in the 1980s and during their post-Freddie Mercury days).

When not busy cranking out guitar solos, he co-runs a company called P1, 'the most exciting prestige and performance car club in the world' (source: P1), and for a while had his own TV programme, *Damon Hill's Wild and Whacky Races*.

VERDICT: TRUE

Damon Hill has also guested on a number of TV comedy shows, such as *Bang! Bang! It's Reeves & Mortimer*.

Lord Byron wrote a poem about ketchup

IT'S DIFFICULT TO picture the 'mad, bad and dangerous to know' Lord Byron – who kept a bear in his rooms at Trinity College, Cambridge – being moved to write poetry after smacking the end of a bottle of ketchup over a plate of fries. Anyone hoping to discover 'Ode to a Ketchup-Bottle' or 'Lines on Hearing that the Restaurant was out of Tomato Sauce' will be disappointed.

The poem in which Lord Byron *mentions* ketchup is the lengthy *Beppo: A Venetian Story* (contrary to indications, this is not a lost Marx Brothers movie). In the eighth stanza, the poet recommends that English visitors to Venice during Lent should stock up on 'Ketchup, Soy, Chili-vinegar, and Harvey' due to the punishing 40-day diet of nothing but sauceless 'ill-dressed fishes'. But *Beppo* could hardly be regarded as a poem *about* ketchup – unless you consider *Oliver Twist* to be a novel about porridge.

The 'Harvey' that appears alongside the ketchup in *Beppo* refers to a popular type of fish sauce – and this is where Byron really did send his 'condiments to the chef'. In 1811, in a now-lost letter to Augusta Leigh, he wrote an epigram humorously comparing the sauce with the English theologian James Hervey: 'The Composite Merits of Hervey's Fish Sauce and Hervey's Meditations'.

Interestingly, Harvey's (or Hervey's) fish sauce does contain mushroom ketchup as an ingredient, but Harvey's is not itself ketchup; so the claim that 'Byron wrote a poem about ketchup' is, unfortunately, not quite true.

VERDICT: FALSE

A more recent poetic usage of 'ketchup' appears in John Betjeman's *Lake District*, where he namechecks 'Heinz's ketchup', as well as 'H.P. Sauce'.

Steely Dan are named after a dildo

THE LEGENDARY JAZZ–ROCK/ROCK–JAZZ band Steely Dan (just 'The Dan' to their hardcore devotees) re-formed in 1995 after a fourteen-year hiatus and are officially still going, but they are best known for their intricate studio albums of the 1970s. At the band's heart is the partnership of Donald Fagen and Walter Becker, who decided to form their own group in 1972. As big fans of 1950s Beat writers, they took their name from a characteristically explicit section of William Burroughs' novel *Naked Lunch* that describes the use of dildos from Yokohama named Steely Dan I, II and III (also referred to later in the book as Danny Boy).

Steely Dan themselves have inspired names used by other artists. The Scottish band Deacon Blue, for example, took their name from 'Deacon Blues', a track from the 1977 album *Aja*. The Dan's 1974 song 'Barrytown', meanwhile, was used as the name of the fictional Dublin suburb in Roddy Doyle's novels *The Commitments*, *The Snapper* and *The Van* ('the Barrytown trilogy') as well as *Paddy Clarke Ha Ha Ha*. The song may have been a direct reference to Barrytown in New York state, near where Becker and Fagen went to university, which was home to the Unification Church ('the Moonies'); it's not clear whether Roddy Doyle realised this when he used the name (potentially lending it extra symbolic weight). On the other hand, all Steely Dan songs are supposedly about drugs, so the lyrics 'I can see by what you carry that you come from Barrytown' may be about heroin rather than the bunches of flowers sold on street corners by Unificationists.

VERDICT: TRUE

The completely unrelated band Steeleye Span are named after a character in the Lincolnshire folk song 'Horkstow Grange'.

Eugene O'Neill disowned his daughter because she married Charlie Chaplin

THE AMERICAN PLAYWRIGHT Eugene O'Neill could accurately be described as a literary heavyweight – and for once, this isn't just a thinly veiled way of calling someone fat. He won four Pulitzer Prizes and the Nobel Prize for Literature, drawing inspiration from the likes of Aeschylus, Nietzsche, Chekhov, Ibsen and Strindberg in thought-provoking, despair-laden works such as *Mourning Becomes Electra*, *The Iceman Cometh* and *Long Day's Journey into Night*. His tragic, disillusioned characters are a far cry from the shoe-eating antics of Charlie Chaplin's pratfall-prone Little Tramp, although Chaplin's artistry and cultural impact were certainly profound.

When Chaplin wanted to marry O'Neill's daughter Oona, Eugene's problem was not with the Englishman's bow-legged walk, silly moustache or any lack of soul-searching in his creative output – quite simply, Chaplin was old enough to be her father. When they met in 1943, Oona O'Neill was seventeen while Chaplin was 54 (only about six months younger than Eugene) and currently embroiled in a paternity suit brought by the actress Joan Barry, herself only 22. Chaplin had something of a penchant for younger women and Eugene, though not exactly a saint himself, was having none of it. He vowed never to speak to his daughter again if she married Chaplin – which she promptly did.

Chaplin's third marriage (or his fourth – depending on whether he really married Paulette Goddard or not) actually proved to be his last and longest. The couple remained an item until his death in 1977, having eight children together. After her husband died, Oona O'Neill Chaplin struggled with depression and alcoholism for the rest of her life.

VERDICT: TRUE

Eugene O'Neill lightened up just once, in 1932, when he wrote a comedy called *Ah, Wilderness!* – his only known use of the exclamation mark.

Brian Jones died in the swimming pool of children's author A.A. Milne

BRIAN JONES FOUNDED The Rolling Stones together with Mick Jagger and Keith Richards in 1962, but by June 1969 increasing problems with alcohol and drugs led to his being fired. (You *really* know you're overdoing it when you get chucked out of The Rolling Stones for living too decadent a lifestyle.) Less than a month later he was found dead in a swimming pool. It did indeed belong to the creator of Winnie-the-Pooh, although not at the time of Brian Jones's death – so it's not as if the ex-Rolling Stone had been downing tequila slammers with Piglet and Eeyore on the night in question.

Alan Alexander Milne, his wife Daphne – real name Dorothy – and their son Christopher Robin moved into Cotchford Farm in Hartfield, East Sussex, in 1925 and on Christmas Eve he published a story called 'The Wrong Sort of Bees' in the *London Evening News*, which would become the first chapter of *Winnie-the-Pooh* the following year. The Pooh stories are set in the area around Hartfield, and while some of the names were changed (to protect the innocent, perhaps), locations such as Poohsticks Bridge and Galleon's Lap can still be visited today.

A.A. Milne died in 1956, but it was over a decade later that Brian Jones quite literally 'bought the farm'. He was busy having Cotchford Farm renovated when he died in suspicious, conspiracy-theory-inducing circumstances.

VERDICT: TRUE

Winnie-the-Pooh's name (whose hyphens were removed when

Disney acquired the rights to the bear) came from a swan called Pooh (namechecked in *When We Were Young*) and a female bear cub named Winnie (short for Winnipeg, her owner's home town), who had been the mascot of the Second Canadian Infantry Brigade before being moved to London Zoo.

Paul McCartney owns the rights to *Rupert the Bear*

LET'S GET ONE THING STRAIGHT: it's officially Rupert Bear (parents: Mr and Mrs Bear), not Rupert *the* Bear.

Rupert was created in 1920 when Lord Beaverbrook, the owner of Britain's *Daily Express* newspaper, decided he needed a comic strip (following the eternally single-minded, originality-stifling spirit of the newspaper industry, the thinking was: if the others are doing it, so must we). The illustrator chosen for the job was Mary Tourtel. She had the advantage of being married to an editor on the paper, though she was already an established children's illustrator and had achieved a degree of fame as a pioneering aviator.

Despite Rupert's origins in hard-nosed boardroom warfare, the bear with the checked trousers became a much-loved institution in the newspaper itself and in spin-off books and annuals. Happily for Lord Beaverbrook, the bear also blew his rivals out of the woods: the *Daily Mail*'s Teddy Tail and the *Mirror*'s Pip, Squeak and Wilfrid probably now reside under a patio somewhere in Nutwood Village. Rupert, meanwhile, was drawn from 1935 by Alfred Bestall, who introduced the distinctive red jumper but stormed off in an Elton John-style tantrum 40 years later, when the *Express* brought out an annual cover on which Rupert's face had been changed from brown to white.

In 1984 celebrated bear fanatic Paul McCartney released 'We All Stand Together' and the accompanying animated 'featurette', *Rupert and the Frog Song*. However, Express Newspapers retained the Rupert Bear rights (after a legal wrangle with Canadian TV company Nelvana) until 2005, when a two-thirds stake was acquired by Entertainment Rights, who also own Postman Pat and He-Man. Here's hoping Rupert will be able to help finally banish Skeletor for good and restore an efficient postal service to Castle Grayskull.

VERDICT: FALSE

On 9 September 1981, following Norway's 2–1 victory over England, 'Loooord' Beaverbrook was commemorated in Norwegian football commentator Bjørge Lillelien's classic 'Maggie Thatcher, your boys took a hell of a beating!' outburst.

Paul Simon's song 'Mother and Child Reunion' was written after he was in a restaurant and saw a dish consisting of chicken with an egg on top

THIS REGGAE NUMBER was Paul Simon's first single after leaving his partnership with Art Garfunkel (who wanted to fulfil the ambition of a lifetime by setting up a chain of restaurants based around a salad-bar theme), and appeared on his first solo album, the imaginatively titled *Paul Simon*, released in 1972.

In an interview that year with Jon Landau for *Rolling Stone* magazine, Paul Simon went into some detail about the song's lyrical content. He explained that after his dog was run over, he realised how deeply the death had affected him, and started thinking about how he would feel if his wife were to die. On the strength of this, Paul Simon must be any psychoanalyst's 'dream patient'.

Paul (or, more fomally: Simon) confessed that he wasn't entirely certain how the title could be interpreted in relation to the rest of the song; and this is surely because, as he had just explained in his answer to Landau's previous question, he'd seen a chicken-and-egg dish listed as 'Mother and Child Reunion' on a Chinese restaurant menu and thought that the name of the dish was so great that he would have to use it as the title for a song. So in understanding the genesis of the song, it's not so much a case of 'Which came first, the chicken or the egg?' as 'Which came first, the chicken-and-the-egg or the dead dog?'

VERDICT: NEAR ENOUGH TO THE TRUTH

Whether the dish specifically had a whole egg on top of some chicken is not absolutely proven; the 'Mother and Child Reunion' dish has been known to comprise shredded chicken mixed up with chopped egg.

Chevy Chase used to be in Steely Dan

THE AMERICAN COMEDIAN Chevy Chase rose to fame in 1975 as one of the original writers and cast members of *Saturday Night Live*, before carving out an incredibly patchy film career. But did he start out in rock–jazz/jazz–rock band Steely Dan before being tempted by the bright lights of *Caddyshack*, *National Lampoon's European Vacation* and *Fletch*?

He studied at Bard College in Annandale-on-Hudson in the 1960s, at the same time as Donald Fagen and Walter Becker, but by that stage Becker and Fagen had not yet formed Steely Dan. They did, however, play in a number of college bands, such as The Leather Canary and The Don Fagen Trio. Chevy Chase played drums a few times in The Leather Canary – which he described as 'a bad jazz band' – but that was it. The Leather Canary weren't and didn't really 'become' Steely Dan, since Becker and Fagen joined Jay and the Americans and then attempted a career as professional songwriters before deciding to form the dubiously named Steely Dan (see p. 88).

Chevy Chase did have another shot at musical stardom, however, playing in a psychedelic pop band called Chamaeleon Church, who released a self-titled LP in 1968 (re-released in 2000). Later in his career he would lip-sync in the video for Paul Simon's 'You Can Call Me Al', sing in the choir for the 'Voices That Care' single for the US troops, and appear in the video for Paul McCartney's theme song to his tedious film *Spies Like Us*.

VERDICT: FALSE
While at Bard College, Chevy Chase went out with Blythe

Danner (Gwyneth Paltrow's mum in real life, and Ben Stiller's future mother-in-law in *Meet the Parents*).

The 'E.' in Richard E. Grant doesn't stand for anything

IT IS ILLEGAL TO CONDUCT an interview with the actor Richard E. Grant, who first rose to fame in 1988's *Withnail and I*, without asking him what the 'E.' stands for. Quite why this is the case is a little mystifying: it's not as if showbiz reporters spend their whole time asking Michael J. Fox what the 'J.' stands for. (If they did, they'd discover that his real middle name is Andrew, but he adopted the 'J.' as a tribute to another actor, Michael J. Pollard.) It's perhaps because Brits are, on the whole, less inclined to tout their middle initials than Americans, so publicly using your middle initial is interpreted as a declaration of eccentricity: 'Hey, look at me: I'm using my middle initial!'

Richard E. Grant was born to British parents in Swaziland, as Richard Grant Esterhuysen. But to the question about 'E.', he has given a fairly consistent answer over the years: it is not inspired by his surname, but was an arbitrary choice when he joined Equity, the British actors' union. When you join Equity, you have to choose a unique professional name. So even if your real name is Richard Grant, you can't join Equity as Richard Grant if someone going by the name of Richard Grant is already a member – even if *their* real name is Bob Holness. In this respect, Equity have elevated their members above Alfred Hitchcock's designation of actors as cattle, to the status of bizarrely named racehorses. This is not

Equity's only odd rule: if you want to stop being a member, you have to pay £25, under a system known as 'honourable withdrawal', which sounds like something you might get taught about in a convent.

It's not clear which Richard Grant was already an Equity member when Richard E. Grant added the 'E.' In at least one interview, Reg, as his friends call him after his initials, claimed that he added the 'E.' to avoid confusion with an American actor, which seems a little unlikely for a British actors' union. But Reg got away lightly: nowadays Equity's application form states that you can't even have a professional name which is *similar* to that of an existing member, and they specifically rule out the addition of a middle name or an initial.

VERDICT: TRUE
The 'S.' in Ulysses S. Grant – no relation – doesn't stand for anything, either: he was born Hiram Ulysses Grant but was mistakenly given his mother's maiden name, Simpson, as his middle name.

None of the cast of *USA High* has ever been to France

FOR THOSE WHO'VE HAD the good fortune never to see it, *USA High* is a 'teen sitcom' in which a bunch of schoolkids are studying at the American Academy in 'Paris, France'. Or at least that's what we're supposed to believe, as indicated by the atrocious 'European' accents, unconvincing backdrops of the 'French countryside' and liberal doses of stock footage.

So that's the 'sit'; in case you were wondering, there is no 'com'. It's so bad it makes *My Family* look like a devastatingly witty slice of Oscar Wilde; yet somehow an astonishing 96 episodes were made. The whole thing seems eerily reminiscent of *Saved by the Bell* – almost as if producer Peter Engel and his collaborators took the same idea and simply transported it to France to make a 'new' sitcom. Not surprisingly, that's exactly what they did – except that they visibly didn't even make it as far as Paris, Texas.

It's standard practice to make TV programmes and films in locations other than the supposed setting (New York sitcom *Friends* was shot in California, for example), but it's *USA High*'s blatant disregard for anything approaching credibility that forms the basis for this claim – as if the show was so excessively non-authentic that even in real life, the actors involved have never been to France and instead assume that French people actually pay in American dollars.

So, who's been to France? An obvious guess would be James Madio (Bobby 'Lazz' Lazzarini), who was in the mini-series *Band of Brothers* – partly set in France, but filmed entirely in England. More definitely, the Dutch actress and former Miss Universe Angela Visser (Miss Dupre in *USA High*) filmed in Paris for real when making the conceptually challenging *Killer Tomatoes Eat France!* – which gives a similarly one-dimensional view of French culture for 'comedy' purposes.

VERDICT: NUL POINT

One wonders whether Gene Hackman or any of the other actors in *The French Connection* ever visited the USA.

Delia Smith baked the cake on the front of The Rolling Stones' *Let It Bleed* album

ALTHOUGH DELIA SMITH later made her name as a TV chef and became Britain's best-selling cookery author, in the 1960s she had numerous jobs, working as a hairdresser, a make-up artist and a shop assistant. Of course, she also landed a job in a restaurant – the Singing Chef – where she worked her way through the ranks, from doing the washing-up to waitressing and eventually preparing food.

By the time she started writing for the *Daily Mirror* in 1969, Delia was also working as a home economist, an occupation that nowadays would be regarded as 'food stylist'. One of her first commissions was to bake a cake that would be photographed by Don McAllester for the *Let It Bleed* cover. The cake is shown speared atop a collection of circular and no doubt foul-tasting items: a tyre, what looks like a pancake or a shammy leather, a clock face, a can of film and, self-reflexively, an LP of *Let It Bleed* itself. If this concept – designed by Robert Brownjohn – doesn't make any sense, it's probably because the album was originally going to be called *Automatic Changer*,

which makes the random selection of round items on a record-changer slightly more comprehensible. Oh, and the shammy leather turns out to be the edge of a pizza, visible on the back cover when the record has been trashed and a large slice of the cake has gone AWOL.

In Bill Wyman's book *Rolling with the Stones*, Delia recalled that the cake was supposed to be 'very over-the-top and as gaudy as I could make it'. The desired effect was certainly achieved – not that The Rolling Stones would have noticed, since they were too busily involved in baking of an entirely different variety.

VERDICT: TRUE
Sadly, in 1973 the photographer David Bailey rather than Delia Smith was called upon to create the cover for the delicious-sounding *Goats Head Soup*.

Bob Dylan now sells most of his records through Starbucks

IF YOU THOUGHT Starbucks was just an overpriced coffee shop named after a character in *Moby-Dick*, think again. In 1999 the Seattle-based coffee company (who also took over The Seattle Coffee Company in 1993, perhaps just to avoid confusion) bought Hear Music, thereby acquiring their own record label and a means to flog exclusive CDs through their 'media bars' and drinks outlets.

In August 2005 Starbucks started selling Bob Dylan's CD *Live at The Gaslight 1962*, under an eighteen-month exclusive deal.

The album contains recordings made, ironically, at a café in Greenwich Village called The Gaslight, when Dylan was on the verge of hitting the big time. Bootleg versions of the songs, primarily traditional folk numbers but with a few Dylan originals, had been circulating for years before Columbia Records' official release was distributed through Starbucks. Clearly many units were shifted, along with plenty of copies of the *No Direction Home* soundtrack shortly afterwards – but equally clearly, Dylan does not sell 'most of his records' through Starbucks.

Even though other artists of his generation have done deals with the coffee company (Joni Mitchell and The Rolling Stones have both put their names to Hear Music's *Artist's Choice* collections), Dylan seemed to attract particular criticism because of his reputation as the seminal anti-establishment songwriter, attacking the evils of capitalism in songs such as 'It's All Right Ma (I'm Only Bleeding)'. News of the deal was therefore a gift to headline-writers and Dylan commentators everywhere, wheeling out excruciating puns like 'Latte on the tracks', 'Everybody must get coffee', 'Ballad of a skinny latte', 'One more cup of coffee (latte to go)' and – well, insert your own pun here.

VERDICT: FALSE
A quarter of all copies of Ray Charles's posthumously released *Genius Loves Company* album were sold through Starbucks.

The Beach Boys wrote the music for *Fawlty Towers*

WOULDN'T IT BE NICE . . . if the instantly recognisable string-quartet theme to the classic British sitcom was written by the laid-back pioneers of Californian pop? Well, for the record, this claim is completely untrue.

The theme music *was* written by a Dennis Wilson – but not *the* Dennis Wilson of The Beach Boys. The *Fawlty Towers* Dennis Wilson was an English pianist and composer who also wrote sitcom theme tunes for *Till Death Us Do Part* and *Rising Damp*, as well as some of the incidental music for the later episodes of *Steptoe and Son*. Confusingly, as well as not being the heavy drinker out of the Beach Boys, he was also not Dennis Main-Wilson, who was one of the producers of *Till Death Us Do Part* and who also produced the unsuccessful series *Mr Big*, which gave Prunella Scales something to do in between the two seasons of *Fawlty Towers*. Finally, Dennis Wilson was also not the Dennis Wilson who played trombone with Count Basie.

After teaching at Ivor Mairants' jazz-heavy Central School of Dance Music in London, 'the' Dennis Wilson became an arranger, composer and pianist at BBC Light Entertainment under the direction of Ronnie Hazlehurst, where he would 'test drive' various prospective TV theme tunes on the piano. He died in 1989.

VERDICT: FALSE

God only knows what the Californian musicians would have made of the beach at Torquay.

Billy Ocean was born in Brick Lane

THE EAST LONDON STREET FAMOUS for its curry houses – recently marketed as Banglatown by tourism bigwigs – does not seem a likely starting point for the singer of 'Caribbean Queen'. Then again, you wouldn't expect to discover that Bruce Willis was born in the German town of Idar-Oberstein, or that Bob Holness was born in the Swiss resort of Davos. (Okay, so that last bit was made up.) Being born 'in' Brick Lane itself sounds a bit suspect. The nearest hospital is Whitechapel's Royal London, on Mile End Road, so presumably either his mother lived on Brick Lane itself, or he was born in an impromptu delivery outside Nazrul.

Not surprisingly, Billy Ocean was not born in Brick Lane. He started life in Fyzabad, Trinidad, as Leslie Sebastian Charles, but when his family moved to London in 1958, they settled in the East End. He went to school in Stepney Green before taking a tailoring course at college, and was then apprenticed to a tailor just off Brick Lane. So *he spent some time in Brick Lane around the age of seventeen*. That doesn't count as being born there, even by pub-fact standards.

Next he worked in the more prestigious West End location of Savile Row, but by 1971 he'd released his first single (as Les Charles). He was later fired from the tailor's (proving that when the sewing gets tough, the tough get going) and worked for a year at the Ford plant in Dagenham, before hitting no. 2 in 1976 (now as Billy Ocean) with 'Love Really Hurts Without You'. The rest, as they say, is R&B.

VERDICT: FALSE

If Billy Ocean's birthplace of Fyzabad sounds like it should be in

Asia, that's because it was named after the Indian city of Faizabad, near Ayodhya (as opposed to Feyzabad in Afghanistan).

Charles Dickens drank a pint of champagne a day

A CENTURY BEFORE James Brown, Charles Dickens could claim to be the hardest-working man in show business. Best known for his novels, he was also a writer of short stories, travelogues and comic plays; a newspaper and journal editor; a theatre producer and actor; and a campaigner on social issues. When it came to popularising literature, he pretty much invented show business.

In 1858, by now an A-list celebrity on both sides of the Atlantic, he took his fame to the next level by inventing the concept of the speaking tour. Earlier public readings for charity had proved so successful that he decided to start speaking publicly as a commercial venture. He toured England, enjoying a great reception and great profits, before taking the show on the road to try to break America.

Dickens invested a huge amount of energy in his public readings, and he began to feel the strain, not helped by the turmoil in his personal life. He had separated from his wife Catherine amid rumours of an affair with Catherine's sister Georgina and, more significantly, with the actress Ellen Ternan, who is said to have remained his mistress for the rest of his life.

To address his declining health, Dickens was recommended to follow a diet that would certainly not be prescribed today, unless you sought medical advice from Dr Thirsty. Before getting out of bed, he had a tumbler of cream and a tablespoon or two of rum. At noon, a sherry cobbler and a biscuit. At three o'clock he downed a pint of champagne. At five to eight, before a reading, he drank an egg beaten up in a glass of sherry. Finally, because it's important to have a balanced diet and not just drink liquid all the time, he would wrap the day up with beef tea and soup.

VERDICT: TRUE, FOR A WHILE
Charles Dickens believed in spontaneous human combustion – perhaps because his constant alcohol intake made his breath dangerously flammable.

Ted Danson's contract stipulated that the *Cheers* bar had to be installed inside his house once the show finished

TED DANSON PLAYED Sam Malone in every episode of *Cheers*, and by the end of its eleven-year run he had negotiated the highest pay packet of any of the sitcom's stars. As someone crazy enough to appear in not one but two films with Steve Guttenberg, it's entirely believable that he would have insisted on a 'set installation' clause. After all, is there anyone alive who wouldn't feel a glow of pride in being able to serve guests a cold beer from the 'real' *Cheers* bar? Your own house, of course, really is a place where everybody knows your name.

The exterior of the 'real' *Cheers* bar was in fact the Bull and Finch pub in Boston, now a tourist attraction known as Cheers Beacon Hill. The inside was a set at Paramount Studios, although in 2001 a replica bar (Cheers Faneuil Hall) was set up in Boston; and by that time Cheers London had opened. Cheers London is also a replica, albeit with the addition of nauseatingly intrusive wall-projected TV screens blaring out live sports; in other words, not somewhere you want to take Aunt Patricia for a spot of afternoon tea. The real-life interior of the Bull and Finch, meanwhile, was actually made to order in England before being shipped to Boston for assembly in 1969.

Ted Danson fans may be disappointed to learn that the interior set was *not* shoehorned into his living room. You can, however, pay it a visit, as it now resides at the Hollywood Entertainment Museum on Hollywood Boulevard.

VERDICT: FALSE

The complete Bag End set from *The Lord of the Rings* films really is installed in director Peter Jackson's backyard.

Frank Zappa made his band play a song about how boring they were

YOU CAN PICTURE THE SCENE. It's 1974, it's 2.30 p.m., and members of the latest incarnation of the Mothers of Invention have turned up at the rehearsal studio. Everyone has arrived on time, because they're so boring. Frank Zappa exhales a cloud of cigarette smoke and says: 'Okay guys, good work last night at the Roxy. Now, I've got a new song I'd like us to play tonight. It's about how boring you all are, and it goes a little something like this . . .'

Would any band ever agree to play a song about how boring they were? Not if they knew that's what it was about – and in the case of the Mothers, they didn't. Zappa's song 'Po-jama People' was played live by his band during 1974, before the studio version was recorded for the *One Size Fits All* album in 1975; its lyrics were sung by Zappa himself, allowing him to express sentiments such as 'The pyjama [*sic*] people are boring me to pieces' and 'They make me feel like I am wasting my time'.

In a 1976 *NME* interview Zappa described his 1973 band as being 'genuinely boring people' and later said that 'Po-jama People' was written about 'the most boring band' he'd ever had to work with. The various line-ups of Zappa's bands changed so much over the years that it is difficult to pinpoint the exact musicians he had in mind, although he did specifically mention percussionist Ruth Underwood and keyboard player George Duke – both of whom appear on the *One Size Fits All* recording.

VERDICT: TRUE
In 1986 Frank Zappa played a drug baron in *Miami Vice*.

When they remade Fawlty Towers for America, they got rid of the Basil Fawlty character

RATHER DEPRESSINGLY, 'they' have actually remade *Fawlty Towers* for American viewers no fewer than three times.

Snavely was screened in 1978 – before the second and final series of the British original – but only made it to a pilot before being dumped. The Basil character was motel owner Henry Snavely, played by Harvey Korman (*Blazing Saddles*' Hedley Lamarr).

The next attempt was *Amanda's*, and here it's probably fair to say that the Basil character *was* eliminated. In a 'hilarious' gender-reversal the lead role was played by Bea Arthur. While her character could in some aspects be compared to Basil – an acerbic hotel owner who is constantly frustrated by the inconvenience of having to cater for guests – part of what defined Basil was the vituperative interplay with his wife; but for Amanda there was no equivalent character. After three episodes in 1983 'they' canned *Amanda's*.

'They' tried again in 1999 with *Payne*, this time retaining a more recognisable Basil Fawlty in John Larroquette's 'hilariously' named Royal Payne. This time 'they' managed to film nine episodes – although the series was cancelled before the last one was screened.

In 2001 BBC Worldwide licensed the format for the first ever non-English version of the series. In planning the German remake, *Hotel zum letzten Kliff*, 'they' set out to be reasonably faithful to the original (with a Basil character called Viktor Stein), although the 'Germans' episode was to be omitted.

VERDICT: ABOUT ONE-THIRD TRUE

There was also a British 'pre-make': the original inspiration for Basil — a character based on Donald Sinclair, who ran the Gleneagles Hotel in Torquay where the Monty Python team once stayed — first appeared in a 1971 episode of *Doctor At Large*, 'No Ill Feeling', scripted by John Cleese.

Margaret Atwood invented a remote-controlled pen

CANADIAN AUTHOR MARGARET ATWOOD IS a busy woman. As well as gaining acclaim for novels such as *The Handmaid's Tale*, *The Robber Bride* and *The Blind Assassin*, she has written poetry, short stories, television screenplays, children's books, non-fiction and literary criticism, and has edited a number of anthologies. With all this work comes the double-edged sword of book tours: a chance to meet fans and sign copies, thereby boosting sales; but also, in her case, exhausting round-the-world travel and a hectic schedule.

Having presumably tried and failed to invent a time machine and a teleportation system, Atwood settled on what she calls the LongPen. Not a very catchy name, although perhaps the original prototype comprised lots of soft-drink straws plugged together with a pen inserted into the end. The final creation is a bit more high-tech: the author uses a stylus to write on an electronic tablet, while chatting to a fan via video; at the other end, wherever in the world the fan might be, a robotic arm uses a real pen to sign the book.

The LongPen (developed by Unotchit Inc., of which Atwood is

Chairman of the Board) can be adapted to inscribe not just books but CDs and, apparently, hockey sticks. The basic principle involved — a stylus at one end controlling the movement of a pen at the other — sounds identical to the Telautograph patented by Elisha Gray in 1888 and demonstrated at the 1893 Chicago World's Fair.

VERDICT: TRUE

Margaret Atwood is not the only celebrity to have created a special device for autograph-signing: during his tenure as artistic director of London's Old Vic, Kevin Spacey installed an 'autograph flap' in the theatre's stage door, so that he could sign programmes without having actually to meet his fans.

There have been three sequels to *Pride and Prejudice*

THERE HAVEN'T BEEN just *three* sequels to or 'novels inspired by' Jane Austen's classic — it's more like twenty, making the *Police Academy* franchise look like a paragon of restraint and good taste.

The formula is simple: write any old drivel, as long as the title contains 'Darcy' or 'Pemberley', or is called *Something and*

Something. Frances Morgan went for *Darcy and Elizabeth* before following up with a double-keyword banker, *Darcy's Pemberley*. She's not the only author to write her own sequel-to-a-sequel: Linda Berdoll republished *Mr Darcy Takes a Wife* (presumably after realising that its original title, *The Bar Sinister*, failed the naming criteria), and then brought out *Darcy and Elizabeth: Nights and Days at Pemberley* (which sounds like Jane Austen is getting the *Baywatch Nights* treatment). Pamela Aidan, perhaps inspired by the *Star Wars* model of unit-shifting, has written the *Fitzwilliam Darcy, Gentleman* trilogy of books (*An Assembly Such as This*, *Duty and Desire* and *These Three Remain*), exploring 'a richly satisfying tapestry of Darcy's past and present'.

Then there's *Trust and Triumph* (Norma Gatje-Smith), *Mrs Darcy's Dilemma* (Diana Birchall), *Pemberley* (Emma Tennant), *The Darcys* (Phyllis Furley), *Darcy's Diary* (Amanda Grange), *Darcy's Story* (Janet Aylmer), *The Confession of Fitzwilliam Darcy* (Mary Street), *Desire and Duty* (Ted and Marilyn Bader – not to be confused with *Duty and Desire*) and the dissatisfyingly named *Conviction* (Skylar Burris) and *Excessively Diverted* (Juliette Shapiro).

Letters from Pemberley, the First Year by Jane Dawkins at least exhibits some distinction by being written in epistolary form, like Samuel Richardson's *Pamela*. But there can be no excuse for her follow-up's excruciating title: *More Letters From Pemberley: 1814–1819: A Further Continuation of Jane Austen's* Pride and Prejudice.

VERDICT: TRUE – AND THEN SOME

Please, if you're thinking of writing a sequel, don't. If you hadn't noticed, *it's been done*.

Alfred Hitchcock didn't have a belly button

EVERYONE IS BORN WITH A belly button, or navel, as it marks the remains of the connection between the foetus and its mother's placenta via the umbilical cord. In fact, it's exactly this issue that represents a major theological headache for many artists: if you're painting a biblical depiction of Adam and Eve in the Garden of Eden, they have to be naked, so do you show them with belly buttons or not? To show them with belly buttons is to make them human, but that would imply they had been born to a human mother, rather than created out of dust or fashioned from a spare rib. Yet to show them without belly buttons would look downright weird; although it would confirm that God doesn't have a belly button either, since man was made in God's image. Usual practice is for artists to wimp out of the whole issue by covering up the relevant area with some foliage, a hand or a tress of hair.

Clearly, Hitchcock must have started life with a navel. However, there is eyewitness evidence of his subsequent lack of a belly button, supplied by the actress Karen Black. She has spent years dining out on the tale of how, during the making of his final film, *Family Plot* (1976), she went into Hitchcock's cabin, believing he was upset with her. In fact, she says, he was just feeling ill, and to put her at ease he thought he'd lighten things up with an explanation of how he had no belly button. She was understandably sceptical, so he showed her where it had been 'sewn away' as a result of surgery.

VERDICT: TRUE

Peas have belly buttons too, where nutrients were transferred from the pod's placenta via the funiculus.

Hue out of Hue and Cry went on to become the *Guardian*'s political correspondent

YOU MAY BE DISTRAUGHT TO discover that the pop–jazz/ jazz–pop duo Hue and Cry, whose heyday was in the late 1980s, consisted of two brothers called Pat and Greg Kane; and that at no stage did they try to pass themselves off as being a bloke called Hue and another bloke called Cry. Their name is a reference to the 1947 Ealing comedy called, er, *Hue and Cry*. The phrase 'hue and cry' is itself, of course, an expression describing an uproar – originally, the commotion caused by someone trying to raise the alarm while chasing after a suspected criminal.

So there's no such person as 'Hue out of Hue and Cry'; although, had one of the brothers actually been named Hugh, then 'Hugh and Cry' might have made for a slightly better pun-based band name (except that the other one *still* wouldn't have been called Cry). In any event, by 2001 the business trading as Hue and Cry had gone into receivership – although they made a musical comeback in 2005 by reaching the final of ITV's *Hit Me Baby One More Time*.

The Kane brothers have always been politically active – for example, they recorded a Scottish National Party campaign song. After being appointed Thinker in Residence to Bristol's first Festival of Ideas, Pat Kane joked that their big hit 'Labour of Love' was 'based on Gramsci's theory of politico-cultural hegemony'.

The cerebral Pat Kane has not quite become the *Guardian*'s political correspondent, but he has written pieces on art and cultural criticism for that paper and others, and helped to found (but then resigned from) Scotland's *Sunday Herald* newspaper.

VERDICT: FALSE

In *Hit Me Baby One More Time* Hue and Cry lost out to Shakin' Stevens.

Salman Rushdie came up with 'naughty but nice' as a slogan to advertise fresh cream cakes

EVERYONE LOVES THE IDEA of Salman Rushdie's background in slogan-writing, quite simply because of the contrast between the serious world of highbrow literature, *Midnight's Children* and death by fatwa – and lowbrow advertising, midnight feasts and death by chocolate.

Any aspiring author has to start somewhere and writing advertising copy is a fairly common first profession for novelists. The man who went on to write *The Satanic Verses* and *Shalimar the Clown* worked for the advertising firms Ogilvy & Mather and Ayer Barker Hegemann in the 1970s, while trying to establish a full-time literary career. During this period Rushdie came up with 'naughty but nice' for cream cakes, as well as 'irresistibubble' for Aero chocolate bars and a rather less catchy slogan for the *Daily Mirror* newspaper: 'Look into the *Mirror* tomorrow – you'll like what you see.'

Another novelist who spent time in advertising was Fay Weldon, who promoted British eggs in the 1960s with the slogan 'go to work on an egg' – though she has claimed she was the manager of the campaign in question rather than the creator of the slogan itself. In 2001 she indirectly returned to the world of advertising by publishing *The Bulgari Connection*, under a contract with Bulgari to promote their jewellery at least twelve times throughout her novel.

VERDICT: NAUGHTY BUT TRUE

Two-time Booker Prize winner Peter Carey was so successful as a copywriter that after writing 'You make us smile, Dr Lindeman' for Lindemans winery (still fondly remembered in Australia today) he went on to co-found an advertising agency.

Sophia Loren invented a type of pizza

ITALIAN SCREEN LEGEND Sophia Loren has long been known for her culinary interests. Over the years she has written a number of books wholly or partly devoted to cooking, such as *Eat with Me*, *Sophia Loren's Recipes & Memories* and the not-as-raunchy-as-it-sounds *In the Kitchen with Love*.

Like many chefs, Loren has published a number of pizza recipes, so it seems odd to claim specifically that she 'invented a type of pizza': this suggests something more innovative, as if she was single-handedly responsible for the stuffed crust, the deep pan or the 'eat as much as you can' (granted, this is not strictly a type of pizza, more an eating concept commonly applied to pizza). The claim may also have been boosted by a prank call on the chat show *So Graham Norton*, in which Sophia Loren spoke with a restaurant owner in Italy who was selling a pizza named after her.

One pizza recipe attributed to Loren actually makes very little specification about what sauces, toppings or herbs should be used, leaving it up to your own preferences; but it reveals her 'secret', which is to knead lots of yellow corn meal into the pizza dough. If you regard the use of corn meal as 'invention', then this fact is true. Moreover, if simply coming up with a pizza recipe constitutes 'invention', then Sophia Loren, who showcased her pizza-vending skills in the 1954 film *L'Oro di Napoli* (*The Gold of Naples*), has actually invented *several* types of pizza. In which case, we might as well all strut around bragging about having invented several types of sandwich.

VERDICT: VAGUELY NONSENSICAL

Fans of recipes created by actors may enjoy *The Sinatra Celebrity Cookbook*, which features such intriguing dishes as Angela Lansbury's Famous Power Loaf, Paul Newman's Italian Baked Scrod and Gene Kelly's Potato Sandwich.

Billy Bob Thornton only eats orange food

MUSICIAN-TURNED-ACTOR-TURNED-MUSICIAN Billy Bob Thornton has gained a media reputation as an 'oddball' due to his supposed vampirism, phobia of plastic cutlery and hatred of Benjamin Disraeli's hair. One of the persistent rumours surrounding his eating habits is the notion that he only eats orange food – which, unless food colouring is allowed, would probably restrict him to a diet of carrots, sweet potatoes, butternut squash, pumpkins, papaya, mangoes, apricots and peaches. And oranges.

And the oil that you might see oozing out of a really dodgy lasagne.

Thornton has repeatedly denied the claim – although not very well. In an interview with Amy Wallace for *Esquire* magazine in 2005, he said: 'I have all these reputations: I'm a blood-sucking vampire. I live in a dungeon. I eat orange food. I'm like: No, I don't. Or: Wait a minute, yeah, I do.' He claims that the rumour started simply because an interviewer once noticed that he only had oranges and carrots on his plate. Yet Thornton is no stranger to dietary weirdness: after he moved to Los Angeles in the 1980s, he was once admitted to hospital with a heart condition brought on by malnutrition, as a result of only eating potatoes. This was, however, out of poverty-related necessity rather than oddball-related choice. Since hitting the big time and sorting out his cash worries, he has subsequently said that he needs to drink a couple of shots of wheat grass juice every morning. On the other hand, he's supposedly allergic to wheat.

Although he denies the whole 'orange food' thing, Thornton does claim to suffer from a genuine phobia of antique furniture, a fact that has been referenced on screen in *Sling Blade* and *Bandits*.

VERDICT: FALSE

Billy Bob Thornton was once in a band called Tres Hombres, which was primarily a ZZ Top tribute act.

SCIENCE

A study showed that a bowl of peanuts on a pub bar contained traces of 100 different types of urine

YEAH, RIGHT, THAT'S WHAT 'a study' showed. It was definitely 100 different types of urine on some peanuts, somewhere. Or it was eleven, or twenty; or was it a bowl of mints offered to people on their way out of a restaurant? Or did 'some experts' say that 50 different types of faecal matter were detected in ice-cubes at a golf club?

Whenever the subject of toilet hygiene – or lack of it – comes up, someone will 'quote' a statistic along these lines (adamant that they remember reading it, although they can't actually remember where or when), to demonstrate how few people wash their hands after a trip to the toilet. While hawking *Charlie and the Chocolate Factory* in 2005, Johnny Depp wheeled out a similar 'fact' on *The Tonight Show*, telling Jay Leno that hearing about this study 'will change your life'. Needless to say, Depp didn't give a detailed citation of his source, although he did give the rather precise figure of 27 different types of urine.

So did a study ever actually put the 'p' in 'peanuts'? None seems to have come to light. However, a 2003 study by the UK Health Protection Agency's Specialist and Reference Microbiology Division found that 44 per cent of ice-cubes examined in 413 London pubs, bars and restaurants contained coliform bacteria, passed out of the human body in faeces. Rather more worryingly, tests detected the presence of the potentially deadly *E. coli* bacterium in 5 per cent of the cubes.

By the way, unlike the 'E.' in Richard E. Grant (see p. 96), the 'E.' in *E. coli* does stand for something – *Escherichia* – but 'a study showed' that you should never write it out in full.

VERDICT: NUTS

In 1998 a urine-on-peanuts-in-bar claim on French TV prompted inventor Jacques Robaey to develop his 'Ten Plus' toilet, which locks the user inside until water has been running in the sink for more than ten seconds – the idea being to force you to wash your hands.

Bracken gives you cancer

MAKE NO MISTAKE: the countryside isn't just boring, it's dangerous. Not only is it full of rusty sheds and abandoned cars, but the seemingly most innocuous plant, bracken, can kill. No wonder the sheep are so easily worried (see p. 157).

If you've recently strolled through a patch of bracken, you probably don't have too much to worry about, unless you had to resort to eating ferns for lunch because the countryside is too boring to have any good restaurants, and even if there were any they would stop serving at 2 p.m. The potentially carcinogenic constituent of bracken and other ferns is an unstable glucoside called ptaquiloside (a tongue-twister often abbreviated to PTQ), and is only known to be definitely harmful if ingested: studies have shown it can lead to bladder and intestinal cancer in cows, and can have similar effects on humans. In Japan, where the culinary use of bracken is widespread (particularly fiddleheads, those little unfurling bits at the ends of new fronds), it is thought to be a contributor to the country's high incidence of stomach cancer.

Still, it's not all doom and gloom when it comes to bracken . . . except that, unfortunately, it is. Scientists have discovered that PTQ can enter the water supply when rainfall washes it from the fronds into the surrounding soil, and it is present in the milk of cows that have been overindulging in the stuff – and there have even been suggestions that in late summer, airborne bracken spores could pose a danger to humans.

VERDICT: TRUE

So, it looks like the safest strategy is to avoid eating bracken, give soft drinks a wide berth, and avoid going anywhere near any kind of fern – in short: stay away from the countryside.

You can use gunpowder to season meat

THIS IS ONE OF A number of claims made by Anthony Hopkins' character Charles in the 1997 film *The Edge*. The rather curious action adventure is a collaboration between David Mamet, writer of *Glengarry Glen Ross*, and Lee Tamahori, who later directed the James Bond vehicle *Die Another Day*.

The Edge tells of two men trapped in a Ray Mears-style survival situation, who have to try to make it back to the lodge where the younger of the two, Robert (Alec 'Always Be Closing' Baldwin), has been photographing Charles's model wife for a magazine shoot. Aside from being attacked by man-eating bears, the main conflict stems from the billionaire Charles's suspicions that Robert is having an affair with his wife.

The bookish Charles has a head stuffed full of trivia which he keeps rattling out, to Robert's increasing irritation. In fact, the film might have fared better at the box office if it had been called *Pub Facts: The Movie*. Some of the other gems of wisdom we are treated to include: 'You can make a compass out of a needle and a leaf' and 'If you've got a stitch, you should pick up a round stone.' By the time Charles starts incessantly yammering about how 'you can make fire from ice' (by compacting ice into a magnifying glass to focus the sun's rays), Robert finally breaks down.

As for gunpowder, Charles could have read this advice in Edward S. Farrow's 1881 book *Mountain Scouting: A Handbook for Officers and Soldiers on the Frontiers*. Whilst black powder (saltpetre, sulphur and charcoal) may be tasty, more modern forms of gunpowder are likely to be poisonous.

VERDICT: NOT ADVISABLE

The Edge also features a bear scampering – although not quite running – downhill.

Britain creates enough rubbish in one hour to fill the Albert Hall

THE ROYAL ALBERT HALL in Kensington was opened by Queen Victoria in 1871, in memory of her late husband Albert, the prince consort. Both Victoria and Albert may be turning in their graves now that its role as a world-class venue for musical events (most notably the annual Proms) has been eclipsed by its use as an indication of volume in lazy journalism. In terms of lazy journalists 'putting things in terms the general public can understand', the Albert Hall is to volume what the football pitch is to area, and laying things end-to-end around the earth is to distance. (Lazy journalists, remember what you were taught at Lazy Journalism Academy: for variety's sake, sometimes it is acceptable to substitute the football pitch with Wales, particularly if you are measuring rainforest destruction or melting ice sheets.)

The problem with waste statistics is that they are generally measured in weight rather than volume – which is why the oft-repeated claim about filling the Royal Albert Hall is so vague as to be useless. This is to say nothing of the fact that some authorities on the subject have claimed it's 'every hour' – for example, the UK government's Environment Agency and countless local councils – while others have claimed it's 'every two hours' or the safer 'under two hours' – for example, the otherwise laudable Recycle Now (run by the UK government-funded Waste & Resources Action Programme), who themselves cite as their source the environmental charity Waste Watch, funded in part by the UK government.

The most recent figure cited is that Britain generates 434 million

metric tons of waste per year, which works out at 1,189,041 tons a day, or 49,543 tons an hour. Assuming a combination of different waste types and taking into account average skip sizes and compaction ratios, a realistic conversion rate based on Environment Agency figures is a volume of 3.3 cubic metres per ton of waste, yielding 163,493 cubic metres of stinking garbage per hour.

According to official figures provided by the Royal Albert Hall's management – the horse's mouth itself – the volume of the auditorium is between 3 and 3.5 million cubic feet, so that's between about 85,000 and 99,000 cubic metres. Even at the top end, this suggests that Britain creates enough rubbish in one hour to fill 1.65 Albert Halls. That's one Albert Hall every 36 minutes. Run to the hills – Britain's waste problem is even worse than 'they' say!

On the other hand, the calculations by Waste Watch use a different Environment Agency ratio of 0.85 tons per cubic metre (or 1.18 cubic metres per ton), resulting in a mere 0.59 Albert Halls per hour; and Waste Watch also point out that Defra (the Department for Environment, Food and Rural Affairs) have recently removed agricultural waste (100 million tons) from their annual estimates – so no one really knows how much waste there is anyway, let alone how much space it takes up.

VERDICT: A WASTE OF SPACE

Statistically, UK government funding generates enough rubbish in one hour to fill a million untrustworthy spreadsheets.

The last 5 per cent of any can of beer is saliva backwash

YOU KNOW THAT FEELING: you don't know whose sofa it is you're sitting on or how you got there, some clown has just put ABBA's 'Dancing Queen' on, and you suddenly notice that the can of beer you're drinking, which started out crisp and cold half an hour ago, is nearly empty – and it's distinctly warm and watery. You nearly retch, so you deposit the can on top of the TV on your route back to the kitchen. If you're the person whose sofa it is, the next morning when you clear up, the number of almost-empty beer cans you keep finding discarded around the house – like an Easter egg hunt but with a pulsing headache – seems to bear out the '5 per cent rule'.

This is one of those facts for which no one needs the fussy findings of detailed scientific investigations: you just know it's true. However, empirical research into the subject *has* been carried out, despite the appalling lack of government funding into this important area of drinking science. In a study of fifteen cans of beer consumed in quick succession at a house party (see Dr Thirsty *et al.*, 'Drinking outside the box: the effects of saliva scare stories on gullible boozehounds', *The Journal of Joined-Up Drinking* vol. 23, 2006) measurements carried out on beer-to-saliva ratios made for interesting reading. After half a 440-millilitre can of lager had been consumed, the proportion of saliva backwash was a mere 3 per cent (6.6 millilitres) of the remaining volume of beer. However, once just 22 millilitres (5 per cent) of liquid remained in the can, the entire volume was found to be saliva.

Although more research has been called for in the light of these results (it is believed that the 'ballast' effect of floating cigarette butts was not taken into account, and the authors make no mention of the impact of a '13.5 per cent extra free' 500-millilitre can size) the overall findings were found to back up the previously untested 5 per cent claim.

VERDICT: TRUE

Experts recommend that to avoid the backwash effect, beer should be 'shotgunned' by piercing the can with a compass (okay, technically a pair of compasses) approximately two-thirds of the way down the side, and then opening the ring-pull to effect the egress of the beer from the resulting aperture.

The Bishop of Cyprus runs an asbestos mine

THIS CLAIM IS immediately spurious on the basis that there is no such person as 'the Bishop of Cyprus'. However, there is a defunct asbestos mine – the Amiandos – in Cyprus's Troodos mountain range, that was owned by the Bishopric of Limassol prior to going into receivership. Quite how or why the Orthodox Church ended up owning such a mine is unclear, but Amiandos was the largest asbestos mine in the world, with an estimated 1 million tons of asbestos fibres produced until the facility's sudden closure in 1988.

It is believed that mining had taken place in the area during ancient times: 'amiandos' means 'asbestos' in Greek, although confusingly the classical Greek word 'asbestos' just meant 'inextinguishable', while in modern Greek it means 'quicklime'. Under Roman rule, Amiandos must have been the washing-up capital of the classical world (see p. 217). During the 1930s the Amiandos mine and its associated community employed over 10,000 people and represented the biggest single source of revenue for the island's economy. At one stage there was a massive flying fox, or death slide, transporting asbestos from the mountains down to the port at Limassol.

In 1995 a plan was hatched to reforest the whole site, with the intention of reversing the environmental effects of nearly 80 years of mining, but progress has been slow. Recruiting volunteers to help clean up a disused asbestos mine is probably about as easy as persuading people to drink battery acid.

VERDICT: WHOLLY CONFUSED
In the Central African Republic the Bishopric of Bakouma and Bangassou owns a miniature hydro-electric power station, with the turbine and cabling installed by a priest; it is not known if the resulting power therefore counts as 'holy electricity'.

No lift has ever fallen all the way to the ground as a result of its cable breaking

LIFTS, OR ELEVATORS, plummet to the earth in movies and cartoons, but does this ever happen in real life? The answer is virtually never: lifts have the most reliable safety record of any vehicular system.

It would take a lot to snap a typical lift cable of intertwined steel – and if that did happen after years of unchecked wear and tear, four or more cables are normally used per car, so you'd need to break several before the lift could fall. Then a governor system would gauge the car's excessive speed, automatically causing brakes on the car itself to clamp (or drive a wedge into) the guide rails in the lift shaft.

Many systems also feature devices that ensure that brakes automatically snap into place when electrical power is lost; as well as detectors at the top and bottom of the shaft to prevent a car travelling too far up or down if the normal control mechanism malfunctions. (Unless, of course, you're Willy Wonka, in which case you can throw health and safety legislation to the wind and ram your elevator and its child occupants straight through the roof at breakneck speed.)

Despite all this, there is one notable example of a full plummet. In 1945 a B-25 bomber mistakenly crashed into the Empire State Building. Lift operator Betty Lou Oliver, blown from her post on the eightieth floor, was badly burned, so she was put in an apparently safe lift to be rushed to ground level. However, because of plane-related damage, the cables broke *and* the safety brakes were not fully effective. The car plunged over three hundred metres to the earth. Miraculously, the slight effect of the brakes, the air compression below the lift and a 'spring' effect of broken coiled cables underneath the car all meant that she survived.

VERDICT: FALSE

Betty Lou Oliver holds the world record for surviving the longest fall in a lift.

More calories are burned eating a stick of celery than are gained in the process

THIS FACT HAS gained particular popularity among pub-goers because it suggests a world in which weight can be lost not by physical exercise but by simply eating more food. Ideally, you could remain seated, order a good Bloody Mary, get your vitamin C from the tomato juice, use a stalk of celery as a swizzle-stick, and then smugly gain a slimmer figure by eating it.

The good news is that celery really is a negative-calorie food. Your average stalk contains around 6 nutritional calories, but it is the celery's very high cellulose content that is key: apart from cellulose, celery is mostly water. In other words the calorie deficit is to do with humans' inability to digest cellulose, or roughage, rather than the energy expended in chewing. So while the calorific content of cellulose can be measured using a calorimeter in the laboratory, it cannot be oxidised by the human metabolism.

As you can probably imagine, eating nothing but celery would not be a sensible way to lose weight; you'd be missing out on other vital nutrients and it would make for a pretty tedious lifestyle.

However, dieters still recommend eating plenty of celery because it can make you feel full, so that you don't snack on other 'bad' foods; and every minute crunching celery is of course a minute not spent wolfing down fried peanut butter and banana sandwiches, cheeseburgers or Dilaudid.

As a diuretic, celery can also help with the removal of water from the body, which is perhaps another contributory factor to its god-like status among dieters – although dehydration is not normally recommended as a weight-loss technique.

VERDICT: TRUE
Other negative-calorie foods include lettuce, garlic and asparagus.

You can't fold a piece of paper in half more than seven times

HOW OFTEN HAVE you heard this one? Maybe you even tried it at school, with a big piece of tissue paper, convinced it was possible. Or perhaps you believed that the presenters on *How?* would succeed with a piece of paper the size of the studio. And we all failed – even the kids on *Why Don't You...?* – so it's generally accepted as true.

In 2002 US high-school student Britney Gallivan succeeded in breaking the seven-fold limit, after being set the problem as a 'math' exercise. At first she tried thin materials, and managed to fold a 10-cm-square (4-inch-square) piece of gold foil more than seven times, with the aid of fine tweezers.

But this was cheating: it wasn't really paper. So she decided to go for width instead of thinness. She acquired a 4,000-foot-long

(1.2-kilometre-long) roll of toilet paper (which she ordered
over the Internet for $85), and
in a shopping mall in Pomona,
California, she and her family
set about folding the paper. It
took seven hours – but they succeeded in folding it twelve
times. If you're desperate to
know all the details of the
highly complicated mathematical solution, then you may
wish to read the paper that
Britney published on the subject: *How to Fold Paper in Half*

Twelve Times: An 'Impossible Challenge' Solved and Explained. It's safe
to assume she spent less time thinking up the title for her paper
than she did on the calculations.

VERDICT: FALSE
Origami has since been removed from the Californian 'math'
curriculum.

Talcum powder is mined from the earth

TALC, TALCUM OR (rather more boringly) magnesium silicate
hydroxide is a mineral used in the manufacture of paints,
insecticides, coated paper, chewing gum and heat-resistant

surfaces. However, most people know it as talcum powder, once it has been purified and combined with a couple of other ingredients such as zinc stearate and calcium carbonate.

Talc could be described as a 'chameleon mineral' in that it is rarely found in large crystals, instead forming pseudomorphs of other minerals: in simple terms this means it sneakily nicks another mineral's shape. It can be white, green, pink, red, grey and black, and has the distinction of being the softest rock in the world (and you thought the softest rock in the world was REO Speedwagon).

Most talc is extracted from the earth in open-cast mines, with over five million tons a year being produced worldwide. The world's biggest talc mine is the Trimouns quarry near Luzenac-sur-Ariège in the Pyrenees, a location that gave its name to the company Talc de Luzenac in 1905 (now a subsidiary of the Rio Tinto mining corporation).

VERDICT: TRUE
Talc is to rabbits what garlic is to vampires – they can't stand the smell of the stuff.

You can't set fire to diesel

THIS MAY HAVE ITS ORIGINS in the idea that while diesel can burn, the way it combusts in an engine is different to the way petrol is ignited. Thus the claim conjures up the image of a potentially explosive substance that, curiously, cannot in fact be set on fire.

In a petrol engine (or gasoline engine in American parlance) the piston compresses a mixture of petrol vapour and air, which is then ignited with a spark. The resulting expansion of gas forces the piston back down the cylinder, rotating the crankshaft via the connecting rod. There's a little more to it than that, but you get the idea.

A diesel engine, by contrast, doesn't use spark plugs to trigger combustion. Instead, the piston compresses air to a much greater extent – and hence a much higher temperature – than in a petrol engine. At the top of the piston stroke, the injection of diesel fuel results in auto-ignition, with the same consequences as the spark-ignition of petrol. In other words, petrol is ignited by an external source, while diesel is heated until it self-ignites.

All this is basically irrelevant. Whether you can 'set fire' to diesel under normal conditions (for example, lighting a match near a trail of diesel leaking from a pump, rather than in a compressed air chamber or an oven) depends on its flashpoint: the lowest temper-ature at which a fuel's vapours will form an ignitable mixture with air near the liquid's surface. Depending on the exact type, for petrol the flashpoint is around -45°C (-49°F), so you'd be in all sorts of trouble – but sure enough, for diesel it's around +45°C (+113°F) or higher, so at room temperature you'd be safe (unless your room was in Death Valley, California, the hottest place on earth).

VERDICT: TRUE

Don't try this at home, or anywhere else.

Camel hair brushes are actually made from the tails of squirrels

RELATIVELY FEW PEOPLE find themselves using camel hair brushes in their day-to-day lives, so it's surprising that this fact has such a high repetition value. Nevertheless, it's a staple of websites listing 'fascinating' pieces of trivia. In some cases, you'll be led to believe that camel hair is so called because it was invented by, or first used by, a Mr Camel.

Camel hair can be used to make cloth, coats and (presumably lumpy) rugs. Calligraphers of old did use camel hair in brushes, but with a few rare exceptions, modern-day 'camel hair brushes' use other types of hair because camels are a bit too woolly for practical use. Typical sources of 'camel hair' include a menagerie of hairy or fluffy-tailed animals: oxen, horses, sheep, ponies, goats, badgers, bears and – last but not least – squirrels. So while not all camel hair brushes are made from squirrels' tails by any means, next time you see a squirrel with a noticeably short tail, you may reasonably want to be on the lookout for scissor-wielding squirrel-rustlers in the pay of unscrupulous paintbrush conglomerates.

The existence of Mr Camel is claimed by some brush manufacturers and artists' suppliers and is mentioned in the 1977 book *Fascinating Facts* by David Louis, but the more mundane possibility is that brushes used to be made of camel hair and the name has stuck – in the same way that French fries can be made anywhere but originate from, er, Belgium.

VERDICT: TRUE, SOMETIMES
The word 'squirrel' derives from the Greek for 'shadowy tail'.

Leonardo da Vinci invented the helicopter

THE QUINTESSENTIAL 'Renaissance man', beardy brainbox Leonardo da Vinci is justly famed for the diversity of his work: magnificent paintings, innovative scientific illustrations, detailed engineering studies, anatomical breakthroughs and a Teenage Mutant Ninja Turtle. He also invented loads of stuff. However, many of his inventions were purely theoretical, because although he spent considerable time devising and documenting their intricate details, they were never actually executed in his lifetime – due to financial restrictions, physical impracticality or sheer laziness.

Like the parachute (see p. 185) Leonardo's helicopter is one such theoretical invention that never actually saw the light of day. But would it have worked if the left-handed genius had been able to realise his plans? The design he drew *circa* 1490 differs substantially from the basic idea of modern helicopters, because it was powered by a single continuous 'screw-top' device rather than by individual blades.

Underneath the screw, which would have been about 4 metres (13 feet) in diameter and made of reed, four men would tediously run around a circular platform to rotate the central shaft, the idea being that the machine would rise up due to the corkscrew effect.

Apart from the fact that having to run continuously

in a circle would make it difficult to see where you were going and easy to feel sick, the main flaw with the celebrity vegetarian's scheme was one for which Isaac Newton, some 200 years later, would have laughed Leonardo out of the house: the forward action of the running men would have simply rotated the base of the craft backwards. Then again, Isaac Newton was from Grantham and an apple fell on his head, so Leonardo would have had the last laugh.

VERDICT: ON PAPER, YES – IN REALITY, NO
In 1910 Sigmund Freud described Leonardo da Vinci as 'frigid'.

All vegetarian restaurants are run by cults

THIS SURELY *can't* be true. Yet there is undeniably a general perception that vegetarian restaurants always have some ulterior motive. In other words, a restaurant can't just happen to offer an exclusively vegetarian menu: there's the implication of a shadowy agenda being pushed by the 'dark forces' running the place, such as religious or political beliefs, tie-dying, or devil worship, usually accompanied by an uptight attitude to the sale of alcohol on the premises.

Worryingly, a superficial trip round the vegetarian restaurants of the world – by flipping lazily through the 'vegetarian eating' sections of travel guides – seems to confirm the theory that wherever there are lentils, cults (or something tenuously like them) are not far behind.

In New York there's Bluestockings, an organic vegan café accompanying a radical bookstore and activist centre supporting 'movements which challenge hierarchy and all systems of oppression'; London's Wild Cherry is run by a group of Buddhist women; in Auckland you could eat at The Blue Bird, as long as you're okay with the spiritual teachings of Sri Chinmoy; and in many cities around the world you can dine at Govinda's, run by the Hare Krishna movement.

Let's be honest, though: none of these places could really be regarded as sinister. What gives vegetarian restaurants a much worse name – quite literally – is their frequent association with atrocious puns. Blazing Salads (Dublin), Sacred Chow (New York), Eat & Two Veg (London) and Pulp Kitchen (Toronto) may offer great menus and are certainly not run by cults, but they do painfully follow the food-pun formula. Which is more than can be said for the forcibly named Badde Manors in Sydney.

VERDICT: FALSE

The Café Gratitude restaurants in San Francisco and Berkeley take the whole naming idea to a new level with dishes such as the I AM GENEROUS guacamole, the I AM VIGOROUS live macadamia nut porridge, and (for drag-queen fans) the I AM DIVINE fiery carrot avocado soup.

'Heroin' used to be a trademark

THIS CLAIM, NOT PARTICULARLY UNBELIEVABLE in itself, is eyebrow-raising because of the notion that at one time someone legitimately trademarked – and hence made huge amounts of money out of – a drug that is now regarded as extremely harmful.

The drug we know as heroin, diacetylmorphine, was invented – or, technically, first 'synthesised' – in 1874 by the British chemist C.R. Wright. He had taken to combining morphine with different acids to see what results might be produced; if this sounds an odd way to pass the time, consider it the Victorian equivalent of Googlewhacking. Yet the commercial potential of the substance was not realised by Wright, and this upholds the long-held belief that experimenting with drugs all day is not something naturally associated with a go-getting entrepreneurial spirit.

The man who decided to sell diacetylmorphine to the medical establishment (although not directly to the public) was Heinrich Dreser, oddball head of the pharmacological laboratory at Bayer. The word 'heroin' was registered as a trademark in various countries in 1898, with Dreser choosing the name because early users described the drug's effects as making them feel 'heroic' (*heroisch* in German).

Initially marketed as a cough remedy, it was soon regarded as an all-round 'wonder drug' – good news for Dreser, as he received a share in the profits of any drugs he launched. However, due to a growing number of negative reports, Bayer stopped making heroin in 1913. But Dreser didn't suffer any bad financial side-effects, as by now he was busy getting rich from the sale of aspirin.

VERDICT: TRUE

In 1924, Heinrich Dreser was forced to retire due to health problems that were rumoured to be the result of heroin addiction; he died of a stroke later that year.

Venus is the only planet that rotates in a clockwise direction

IT SEEMS ODD to describe the workings of the universe in terms of that very recent human invention, a clock. And since in reality the solar system is not viewed from afar, as some enormous orrery, who's to say which way is 'clockwise' and which way is 'anti-clockwise'? Surely it depends which way you look at it – which, in reality, you can't.

Let's suppose, for the sake of argument, that you were looking down on the planet from above the north pole. (For the purposes of this experiment, it doesn't matter which of the various north poles you choose – see p. 143.) In that case, Venus does indeed rotate clockwise on its axis – whereas the Earth rotates anti-clockwise. The upshot is that if you were standing on the surface of Venus, you'd see the Sun rising in the west and setting in the east. Except of course, the Sun doesn't actually rise at all. And anyway, you wouldn't be able to stand on the surface of Venus because you'd be crushed to death by the pressure, if you hadn't already been melted alive.

Not only does Venus rotate clockwise, it rotates incredibly slowly, to the extent that a year on Venus is slightly quicker than a day on Venus. If that sounds like it makes no sense at all, think of it like this: it takes longer for Venus to rotate once on its own axis than it does for the planet to orbit once around the Sun.

Despite all this, Venus is not unique in its clockwisdom (if that's a word), because Uranus and Pluto rotate in the same manner.

VERDICT: FALSE
In space, no one can hear you yawn.

Strawberries contain more vitamin C than oranges

YOU MAY HAVE BEEN BROUGHT UP believing that oranges are the best source of vitamin C. While that's not strictly true, don't be too hard on your elders, because it's probably fair to say that it's the most readily available, cost-effective and practical means of obtaining natural vitamin C; and grown-ups don't enjoy using phrases like 'the most readily available, cost-effective and practical means' unless they are management consultants.

When trying to compare how much of a particular nutrient any foodstuff contains, it's always tricky because of differences in what can be sensibly compared. One option is to compare content by mass – even though, in grams, the amount of grapefruit you could eat is considerably more than the amount of hot chilli peppers you could keep down. (Unless, that is, you are Doug Wilkey, who won the 2005 World Championships held by the International Chilli Society, 'a not-for-profit organization that sanctions chilli cook-offs'.) Another option is to compare content per 'standard serving' or 'common measure', based on how much you might normally eat. Other studies provide rankings that take into account different aspects such as calorific value and nutrient density.

Methodology notwithstanding, there are some clear winners over the humble orange. Strawberries do contain slightly more vitamin C, but even richer are redcurrants, papaya, lychees, kiwi fruit, blackcurrants, red peppers (yes, the capsicum is a fruit) and guava. By mass, the fruit with the highest vitamin C content seems to be the rosehip (although there are some extremely rare fruits, such as camu camu, that contain even more).

VERDICT: TRUE

Non-fruit foods that contain more vitamin C than oranges include
Brussels sprouts and broccoli.

If you go to altitude, smoking is good for you

IN THIS DAY AND AGE would anyone seriously suggest that
smoking, under any circumstances, is good for you? This 'fact' con-
cerns mountaineering — although perhaps it's not far from the
equally bogus claim that you should smoke because on long-haul
flights you'll be seated at the back of the plane, where you're more
likely to survive a crash.

Those in the pro-smoking-at-altitude camp may also point out,
having researched the contentious issue of dog-to-human years
(see p. 24), the astonishingly high average life expectancy in
Andorra — a mountainous principality in the Pyrenees that is
noted for its production of cigars and cigarettes. However,
Andorra's high life expectancy is probably due to the fact that
there is no crime, they don't have an army, they haven't been
invaded for a while, the literacy rate is 100 per cent, the state
funds all healthcare and pensions, and everyone is rich enough to
live a life of comfort — no matter how many packets of fags they
get through while out on the piste.

The medical establishment is adamant that smoking is bad for
you, *especially* at high altitudes. Whether you're puffing on a tab or
not, above about 2,400 metres (8,000 feet) the supply of oxygen to
the blood can become insufficient due to the lower atmospheric
pressure, resulting in hypoxia (altitude sickness). Medical advice is

to stop smoking before you start climbing, since carbon monoxide from cigarettes can impair the ability of haemoglobin to transport oxygen. The only sense in which smoking may *appear* to be 'good for you' is if you use a pulse oximeter to measure your blood's oxygen saturation, since it may not be able to tell the difference between oxygen and carbon monoxide – so chain-smoking your way through 40 cigarettes may mistakenly give the impression of superhero-like oxygen levels.

VERDICT: GIBBERISH

There's an ashtray at the top of Mount Everest.

At the end of the day you're three-quarters of an inch shorter than when you got up

CLEARLY, THIS FACT only applies to people who bother getting out of bed in the morning, unlike Florence Nightingale (see p. 214). Assuming you do, you will certainly be a bit taller at the start of the day than when you go to bed.

The amount by which your stature decreases depends on the loading of the spine caused by whatever activities you happen to get up to during the course of the day. To take a typical example, if your job is riding on the bottom row of a motorcycle acrobatics troupe, with a pyramid of lycra-clad, goggle-wearing athletes propped up on your head, chances are you'll lose more than an inch (over 2.5 cm). But a loss of three quarters of an inch, or slightly over 1 per cent of your morning height, is about 'normal'.

Studies have shown that walking causes your height to reduce more quickly than merely standing still, running even more so, and that usually about half of the height loss occurs within the first hour of getting up. Cast-iron logical deduction therefore indicates that to retain height you should stay in bed for an extra hour every morning – unless you're self-conscious about being too tall, in which case you should stay indoors jogging furiously for the first hour. As for putting it back on again, studies indicate that it takes longer, with about half the night's sleep required to regain three-quarters of the height loss, assuming you are lying down rather than participating in some sort of David Blaine sleeping-standing-up prank.

VERDICT: APPROXIMATELY TRUE

Cows, horses and elephants can sleep, or at least power-nap, while standing up.

The earth has three north poles

AMAZINGLY, THERE ARE some numb-nuts out there who still consider themselves 'explorers', having failed to notice that humankind has been everywhere now. In fact, the only real places on earth that humankind hasn't checked out properly are various difficult-to-reach areas of the ocean floor. However, if you're an 'explorer', don't bother exploring those remaining places, because that's actually quite challenging – instead, just keep going back to the tried-and-tested places that everyone else has been to. The thing is, though, now you need a *gimmick*. You've got to be the first man between the ages of 42 and 44 to paddle across the English Channel in a repurposed Victorian toilet; or the first physics teacher to moonwalk solo (unassisted by the sounds of 'Billie Jean') to the top of Mount Everest while wearing a Marty McFly Jr baseball cap. Finally, go on and on about how hard you are, 'braving' the tough conditions, until you get stuck in a snowdrift and have to put other people's lives at risk looking for your idiotic stranded self.

Does this sound like you? If so, before setting out on your useless quest to the north pole, you may be interested to learn that you'll have to figure out *which* of the north poles you're aiming for. If you've already booked your helicopter ticket, don't worry – they're all in the Arctic Ocean (for the time being, anyway).

Magnetic north – where your compass points – is the spot at which the earth's geomagnetic field points vertically downwards, and is moving away from Canada towards Russia at the alarming-sounding rate of 40 kilometres (25 miles) a year. Confusingly, because the north pole of a magnet points to it, magnetic 'north' is technically a south pole, since only opposite poles attract; but let's just stick to calling it magnetic north.

The geographic north pole is where the earth's axis of rotation meets the earth's surface (actually, even this is not a fixed point, due to a variation in the earth's axis known as the Chandler wobble – probably named after some 'hilarious' drunken incident in *Friends*). This point is said to be 'true north', at 90° latitude, so that in whichever direction you head, you're moving south.

Then there's the geomagnetic north pole, which is not the same as the plain old magnetic north. Geomagnetic north is the point where the earth's magnetic dipole meets the surface (imagine a massive bar magnet rammed through the middle of the earth), which turns out to be tilted by about 11° compared to the earth's axis of rotation.

Finally, there is a *fourth* north pole: the northern pole of inaccessibility (also known as the Arctic pole). This is the point in the Arctic Ocean furthest from any coastline.

VERDICT: KEEP COUNTING!

There are even more south poles: four corresponding to the north poles described above (with the pole of inaccessibility being the point on Antarctica furthest from the surrounding oceans), plus the ceremonial south pole: a permanent marker consisting of a small reflective sphere on top of a red-and-white stripy stick (which was probably nicked from a barber's shop by some scientists on a boozy night out).

Tea does not actually contain caffeine, but a very similar substance called teaeine

TEAEINE? This is enough to try anyone's patience! *There is no such word as 'teaeine'.* Understand?

But wait a minute, what's this? The word 'theine', pronounced in the way you'd expect 'teaeine' to be pronounced, is actually a word. That's right: *the word 'theine' exists.* The word was first recorded in English in 1838 (in the form 'theina'), though the substance itself is believed to have been identified in tea in 1827, seven years after the isolation of caffeine by Friedrich (aka Friedlieb) Ferdinand Runge – who started analysing coffee on the suggestion of Johann Wolfgang von Goethe.

It wasn't long afterwards that some wiseguy pointed out that theine and caffeine were chemically identical. So most people stopped using the word 'theine' because it doesn't look very pronounceable, although there is a tea shop called Théine in Coral Gables, Florida, named after the original French version of the word.

VERDICT: FALSE

Caffeine occurring in guarana is called guaranine; in malt drinks it's called Ovaltine.

If you find a new prime number over 100 digits long, the US government will give you $10,000

AS YOU PROBABLY remember from school, unless you were too busy etching 'Shaz snogged Acne Dave' into the desk with a compass, a prime number is a positive integer with two integer divisors: the number 1 and the prime number itself. To put it a bit less precisely but a bit more clearly, it's a whole number that can only be divided by itself and 1. Listing examples starts out easy – 2, 3, 5, 7, 11 and so on – but it would quickly make for a pretty fiendish, and silent, drinking game.

Ever since Euclid first proved in about 300 BC that there are an infinite number of prime numbers, the search has been on to find the biggest number possible. By definition an endless task, the idea is that each time someone finds a prime number bigger than the last one, they rise above day-to-day boffindom and become a mathematical sex symbol, finding themselves knee-deep in integers and calculus, but destined eventually to become embroiled in allegations of three-in-a-set isosceles love triangles.

Finding new prime numbers can prove directly or indirectly useful for the study of cryptography, which is perhaps how this claim about the US government arose – the idea being that big prime numbers allow state secrets to be so highly encoded that a shadowy figure from the CIA will quietly take you to one side and buy the number from you for $10k. This 'fact' also found its way into Mark Haddon's best-selling novel *The Curious Incident of the Dog in the Night-Time* – though as Christopher, the book's autistic protagonist, astutely points out, 'it would not be a very good way of making a living'.

Unfortunately it's not actually true. In fact a much larger prize can be won (for a much larger number) from the non-profit-making Electronic Frontier Foundation's Cooperative Computing Awards – designed to encourage the participation of ordinary Internet users in collectively solving 'huge scientific problems'. If you're the first to find a prime number with at least ten million digits, they'll hand out $100k; over 100 million digits in length and it's $150k; and for the whopping grand prize of $250k you'd need a prime number a billion digits in length.

VERDICT: FALSE

The Clay Mathematics Institute of Cambridge, Massachusetts, is offering a reward of $1 million per solution for solving seven

'Millennium Prize problems'. Your first step to netting the total $7 million prize money would be to understand what the actual problems are, given their rather specialised titles like 'Yang-Mills and Mass Gap' and the deceptively simple-sounding 'P versus NP'.

You can shave with peanut butter

THIS IS AN ABSURDLY POINTLESS CLAIM. You can shave (not necessarily very well) with just about anything that can be smoothed onto the skin, as long as the razor can still move. So Superglue is probably off-limits. Peanut butter is certainly pretty thick but you can use it if you really want to, though for a closer shave it is recommended to use the smooth rather than the crunchy variety, and you should avoid it altogether if you have a massive peanut allergy. You would also have the benefit of a good moisturising effect from peanut butter's high oil content.

The curious prevalence of this fact in trivia lists probably originates in a quote attributed to Barry Goldwater, the former Arizona senator and 1964 presidential candidate for the Republican Party. He is supposed to have said, in reference to a camping trip where he ran out of shaving cream, 'It's a darn good lotion if you don't mind smelling like a peanut.' Goldwater – a man who declared the official food of the United States to be chilli – was known for his outspoken comments and humorous quips, but it's entirely possible that the quote is apocryphal, particularly since a slightly different version is often cited: 'If you don't mind smelling like peanut butter for two or three days, peanut butter is darn good shaving cream.' It's not exactly the funniest of comments, however, which suggests it may have its basis in truth rather than having been invented for comedy purposes.

VERDICT: TRUE

Another reason for the 'spread' of this claim is that best-selling writer and comic Joey Green – who has made a career out of documenting unexpected uses for household products – managed to get Jay Leno to shave with peanut butter on *The Tonight Show*, and performed the same stunt with Rosie O'Donnell's leg.

Mosquitoes have been responsible for the deaths of half of all the human beings who have ever lived

MOSQUITOES CAUSE RATHER more trouble than just an itchy bite and a buzz that sounds like a miniature light sabre. Most of their lethality stems from the fact that various species of mosquito act as carriers of malaria and yellow fever; some also help to transmit dengue, the filariasis worm and various forms of encephalitis. The World Health Organization puts the number of deaths caused by malaria alone to be over a million humans annually; worryingly, in recent years this figure has been on the increase again.

As to whether mosquitoes have been responsible for half of all human deaths ever, it's kind of difficult to know for sure. But it's comforting to think that there's a God up there who's a bureaucratic control freak: you can't get into heaven – and certainly not hell – without having to bring your death certificate with you and fill out a series of multiple-choice questions relating to the cause of your death. God's administrative assistants compile these statistics (crunching the numbers with an antiquated mainframe computer donated by Albert Einstein, as part of a heavenly plea bargain for having invented the atomic bomb), and have concluded that the mosquito holds the status of 'the creation of God most likely to bring other creations of God back to their creator the fastest'.

The 'half of all human deaths' claim, whether for malaria specifically or mosquitoes more generally, is often accompanied by disclaimers such as 'until the 1950s' (to acknowledge the effects of insecticides from that period onwards) or 'not counting wars' (to acknowledge the wide-reaching effects of human idiocy). The compilers of *Guinness World Records*, in their entry for 'most dangerous parasite' (ladies and gentlemen, please swat your hands together for malarial parasites of the genus *Plasmodium*), opt for 'excluding wars and accidents' and 'since the Stone Age' – but even they have to qualify the whole record with the word 'probably'.

In terms of its scholarly origins, the claim has been attributed to Nobel laureate Baruch S. Blumberg, but it appears in various forms at least as far back as 1960. For example, in an article entitled 'Man in a World of Insects', Dwight M. Delong cited 'the world health authorities' for the claim that insects generally are 'the cause of one-half of all human deaths, sickness, disease, and deformity'. It's possible that over the years, this much broader claim became fine-tuned to blame mosquitoes.

VERDICT: IT SUCKS, BUT IT'S BELIEVABLE

In the case of mosquitoes, the female of the species really is more deadly than the male, since it's only the female that sucks blood and transmits the malaria parasite.

If you're the only person who can smell burning rubber, it means you have a brain tumour

LET'S MAKE SOME ASSUMPTIONS HERE, for the sake of allowing this apparently ludicrous claim a fair hearing. First, let's rule out a scenario like that Tom Hanks film, in which your plane has crashed on a desert island, and as the only survivor you're so fed up with having to talk to a basketball that you've decided to set fire to it. In other words, let's assume that there are other people around. Second, let's assume that those other people don't suffer from anosmia, the loss of the sense of smell.

Okay, you're surrounded by able-smelling persons, there's not an accelerating road vehicle in the vicinity, you can't see any flames, and you're the only one who can smell burning rubber. Should you rush off to the nearest medical facility? Possibly, yes, if you heed the story of the composer George Gershwin. On 11 February 1937, at the height of his success and not yet 40, Gershwin complained of being able to smell burning rubber when nobody else could, in the middle of performing his *Concerto in F* at the Los Angeles Philharmonic Auditorium. Exactly four months later, he died of a brain tumour.

Now, let's get this in perspective. Gershwin had a number of other 'warning signs', such as dizzy spells, which nowadays would probably result in earlier, possibly life-saving, treatment – and he refused to undergo a spinal tap to assist diagnosis (if he could only have foreseen the film *This Is Spinal Tap*, he might have changed his mind about the whole lumbar puncture thing). Nevertheless, when it comes to olfactory hallucination (imaginary smells), burning rubber is up there with rotten apples as a relatively common smell reported by patients. It is, in fact, a possible symptom of temporal lobe epilepsy; this could in turn be secondary epilepsy brought on by a brain tumour – but not necessarily. So, if you genuinely find that you're the only person who can smell burning rubber, it doesn't 'mean you have a brain tumour', but it would be a sensible precaution to check with your doctor (after you've checked whether you've left the handbrake on).

VERDICT: FALSE

If you're one of *several* people who can smell burning rubber, you should probably stop standing around chatting about George Gershwin and look for the nearest fire extinguisher.

One cup of anthrax can kill half a million people

ANTHRAX DOESN'T NORMALLY come in cup form – although in November 1999 some 'prankster' at a former uranium processing plant in Ohio left a cup on a desk with an attached note reading: 'Do not touch – anthrax sample'. The 'hilarious' consequences of the hoax involved costly call-outs to the FBI, the Centers for Disease Control and Prevention, and various emergency services.

So let's take a cup to mean a volume of about 240 millilitres (8 fluid ounces) of *Bacillus anthracis* in spore form, prepared by someone with rather sinister intent for release into the atmosphere, where it could be inhaled by humans. (Anthrax could also be spread via the water supply or food, but that would be completely impractical.) Weaponised anthrax has – thankfully –

never been deployed in such a manner to test the half-a-million-people theory, and epidemiologists and bioterrorism experts aren't certain about how lethal any particular large-scale dose might be. There are also many different strains, some highly virulent, others benign; and obviously it depends on where and how the spores are released, and which way the wind is blowing that day. Still, that doesn't stop pub-goers and politicians alike confidently asserting the dangers of 'a cup of anthrax'.

A study by the now-defunct US Congressional Office of Technology Assessment in 1993 suggested that releasing 100 kilograms (220 pounds) of the stuff could result in up to 3 million fatalities; this would mean that for half a million, you'd be looking at about 17 kilograms (37 pounds). That's a pretty big cup – and no, anthrax spores aren't really so heavy that you could fit 17 kilos into 240 millilitres. A report published in the *Proceedings of the National Academy of Sciences* in 2003 estimated that 1 kilogram (2.2 pounds) of anthrax spores dropped on a city of 10 million inhabitants could kill just under a quarter of a million people. Luckily for us, the report's authors decided to use mathematical modelling for their predictions, rather than getting up there in a plane loaded with an anthrax-filled tea service; but it's pretty clear that there is no real evidence for this one-cup claim.

VERDICT: FALSE

Despite being mercifully short, the song 'Cupajoe' by the American metal band Anthrax, which is all about how much they need a cup of coffee, may have bored half a million people to death since being released into the public domain in 1998.

All lifts allow you to travel straight to your floor without stopping, by holding down the 'close doors' button while selecting your floor number

THE IDEA GOES THAT IF you live on the twentieth floor and don't want to have to stop on the way down to the ground floor, just because your neighbours have thoughtlessly called the lift as well, this trick will get you there straight away. Theoretically, if people in the lift with you have selected other floors already, you'll override those too – although you may end up on the wrong end of 'elevator rage'.

Many lifts really do have an 'express mode' of this sort, for use by cleaners or security staff, for example, but it's activated by a key rather than the 'close doors' button. If you care to test it, the 'close doors' theory is pretty easy to disprove, and the major lift manufacturers certainly deny that this 'hack' exists. However, there are those who claim this is because 'they' don't want you to know that the secret code exists, presumably because too much knowledge in the wrong fingertips would lead to a massive crisis of inefficiency in the world's vertical transportation systems, with suitcase-laden hotel guests waiting weeks to get to the ground floor. Which makes you wonder why 'they' would bother providing for such a code in the first place. Nevertheless, the number of anecdotal claims of this technique working is extraordinarily high, so it's possible, just, that certain lift models have the feature enabled. Even if you find it does work, *no one* will believe you until they've seen it with their own eyes.

In fact, conspiracy theorists are particularly zealous when it comes to 'close doors' technology, with many claiming that all 'close doors' buttons actually have no effect whatsoever under normal circumstances. In other words, it's just an unwired placebo button to calm your frustration while waiting for the doors to shut, which doesn't actually close the doors any faster than the normal delay after choosing your floor number. Certainly, many 'close doors' buttons may be disconnected or malfunctioning, but it doesn't take long to find one that works. Which is more than can be said for the 'express mode' combination.

VERDICT: FALSE

If this trick was reliable, then Jack Lemmon might have been born in a lobby (see p. 70).

THE LAW

A farmer has the right to shoot any dog that is worrying sheep

PUBLIC RIGHTS OF WAY OFTEN pass over or near farmland, and the issue of dogs pestering livestock is something of a sore point for many farmers. Even your seemingly harmless little shih-tzu could severely traumatise a sheep by yapping too much, and there's every likelihood of it saying 'boo' to a goose. As a result, farmers have little patience for walkers accompanied by un-controlled dogs – and they're liable to take measures to protect their animals, particularly during lambing season.

Many countries have legislation giving livestock owners the right to pop a cap in your pup if it's vexing their flock. In England and Wales, under the Animals Act 1971, if the owner of the livestock shoots (or in some other way kills or injures) your dog, he or she is perfectly entitled to do so if the dog 'is worrying or is about to worry' the animals and there is no reasonable prevention. In fact, even if your dog has finished worrying the sheep and then has a good roll-around in the grass, the farmer can still shoot the dog if it's not under con-trol and you're not around to claim possession of the pooch.

In New Zealand, a nation of around 40 million sheep, under the Dog Control Act *any* person witnessing a dog attack (against themselves, livestock, domestic animals or protected wildlife) may 'forthwith either seize or destroy the dog'.

In the USA, most states have something along the same lines. In Ohio, the law says that 'a dog that chases, injures, or kills livestock, poultry, other domestic animal, or other animal, that is the property of another person, except a cat or another dog, can be killed at the time of that chasing, approaching, attempt, killing, or injury'. Although clumsily expressed, the message is clear: in Ohio, the authorities blatantly turn a blind eye to dog-on-dog crime, while actively discriminating against cats, who are very much the underdogs in this situation.

VERDICT: TRUE

Leash it or lose it!

If you travel to the USA on a tourist visa and get a job while you're there, you can keep that job

YOU MIGHT HAVE naïvely thought that the point of a tourist visa was to ensure someone could travel to the USA for holiday-making purposes and then, after a fixed amount of time, *leave the country*. Not so, according to pub lawyers. Most people spend their hard-earned holidays seeing the sights and enjoying a break, rather than hunting for jobs; so presumably the idea is that by exploiting this loophole, you avoid the hassle of proper paperwork.

For citizens of countries in the Visa Waiver Program, such as the UK, Ireland, Australia and New Zealand, no visa is required for a tourist visit of up to 90 days. For those tourists who do need a visa, however, it's technically a 'visitor visa' or B-2. To qualify for a B-2 visa, according to US Citizenship and Immigration Services, applicants must provide evidence of their intent to return home after a 'specific, limited period', as well as having a residence outside the US and demonstrating 'binding ties which will insure their return abroad at the end of the visit'.

The rules are clear: 'Persons entering the United States on a visitor or business visa, or under the Visa Waiver Program, are not permitted to work.' There's no option to 'keep a job' once you've got it, because on a visitor visa you cannot legally get one to start with.

What about getting a job – but not actually doing any work? Though admirable, this would still technically be illegal.

VERDICT: NO CHANCE
Incidentally, the Green Card (the document confirming that some-one is a 'Lawful Permanent Resident' of the USA) isn't actually green.

Once a fine is paid or a jail sentence is completed, any conviction is removed from your criminal record after seven years

YOU READ THAT RIGHT: it doesn't matter what level of crime spree you've embarked upon or how many gruesome deeds you've carried out, seven years after you've completed a stretch or paid your fine the authorities need never know about it again. Just because you once did stir for a violent jewel heist doesn't mean you can't get a job looking after a high-security bank vault seven years later: your rap sheet is as spotless as the 'YOU'RE FIRED!' fax at the end of *Back to the Future Part II*.

These days, of course, most countries don't have anything resembling a single 'criminal record', as if there is one long sheet of paper with all your crimes written on it, being reeled off a toilet-roll holder. In reality, the various authorities – police databases, court recorders, and so on – will hold plenty of information about you well after the event. In many countries, even after a conviction is 'spent', some form of police check or criminal records check (for example, by the amusingly named CrimTrac in Australia or the Criminal Records Bureau in the UK) will reveal full details of all indictable convictions – and even some unproved allegations – if an ex-con is applying to work in a school or other position of particular responsibility. Many countries and states implement some form of violent or sex offenders' register that will require offenders to keep authorities updated as to their whereabouts for the rest of their lives.

Most justice systems do provide for a notion of 'spent' convictions and 'rehabilitation periods', following which an offender is for most purposes regarded as above-board again, and certain details are 'weeded' from the records. However, that doesn't mean that *no* records are retained, and the periods involved typically vary depending on the nature of the conviction. In the UK, for example, the rehabilitation period following a custodial sentence of up to six months does happen to be seven years; but for a sentence of between six and thirty months it's ten years.

VERDICT: FALSE

One criminal record that should have been removed by the Police was 1981's *Ghost in the Machine*.

When driving, you can't be booked for speeding unless the police officer is wearing a hat

THIS IS SUCH A LAUGHABLE CLAIM that it barely merits investigation. Wearing 'a' hat presumably means wearing a proper police officer's hat, so they couldn't just coolly amble up to your car wearing a massive sombrero (unless you're speeding in Mexico).

Actually, they probably could, because it doesn't matter where you live, trying to plead 'inappropriate hat style' or 'headdresslessness' as a defence is not going to get you out of a speeding fine. In fact, if you try to argue the case you'll probably find yourself booked for wasting police time and made to walk home wearing a jazz beret.

As long as a police officer is clearly recognisable as such, with a uniform, identification badge, or – and be careful here – a heavy, skull-bashing nightstick or truncheon, you can get done for speeding. The only way out, as any sensible driver knows, is to drive so fast that you cannot be captured on a speed camera.

VERDICT: ABSOLUTE NONSENSE

And yes, you *can* be fined for speeding in a hire car – do you seriously think 'they' haven't figured out how to track you down?

Tower Bridge is the only bridge in the world that counts as a ship for insurance purposes

LONDON'S MOST RECOGNISABLE bridge (you know, the one that American guy thought he was buying when he accidentally ended up having to deposit the 'real' London Bridge in the Arizona desert) was opened in 1894 by the Prince of Wales, who later became King Edward VII.

Tower Bridge, along with the other four bridges that connect the City of London to the south side of the Thames, is managed by the Corporation of London with money from the Bridge House Trust. This charity is a centuries-old institution whose name derives from a building to the south of the first stone London Bridge, where tolls, fines and other revenues relating to the bridge were collected.

Until 1995 the Bridge House Trust's sole purpose was to pay for the construction, upkeep and purchase of bridges, but then they realised they had so much spare cash floating about that they began to administer surplus funds to deserving London-related projects in the form of grants.

Although rumours abound that the bridge is 'insured by Lloyd's of London on the shipping register as a ship', it isn't. The Bridge House Trust point out that if any of the bridges were to collapse, they would have to rebuild them with their own funds — so they keep a cash pot going for just such an eventuality.

VERDICT: FALSE
In 1952 a double-decker bus with several passengers on board was forced to jump the gap between the rising bascules.

Traffic wardens cannot legally touch the vehicle they are ticketing, so you can cover up your number plate with a plastic bag to avoid parking fines

THIS PARKING LOOPHOLE has long been claimed by London's motorcycle couriers, ever wary of being ticketed during the 30 seconds they're dropping off or picking up a package. The theory is that traffic wardens can only touch a vehicle for the direct purpose of applying a ticket — for example, putting it under a windscreen wiper — so any other vehicle contact is forbidden.

This practice has come under scrutiny since it became more widely known. It really did seem to work for many years, probably on a 'let sleeping dogs lie' basis, but in 2004, following claims that fraudster-turned-TV-presenter Lord Brocket was exploiting the scam, Westminster Council told the *Mail on Sunday* that they would now be asking their wardens to remove anything obscuring number plates. No one involved in any aspect of parking will give

you a straight answer, but it's safe to assume that no local authority will let you get away with it now. In any case, if your engine number is visible, a warden can use that instead of your registration number.

You would think that by covering up the number plate, you could be fined for failing to display your vehicle registration details adequately, which is as bad as using italics (see p. 181). While this certainly applies to parking on the public highway, parking on private property (such as a privately owned stretch of pavement) is a nebulous legal area.

VERDICT: FALSE

You definitely can't be fined until a warden has put a ticket on your windscreen – so if you speed off just as it's about to be issued, 'they' can't prove that 'they served the document'.

The Highway Code is not legally enforceable

THIS IS A CLAIM SPECIFIC to the British rules of the road, as embodied in the Highway Code: a booklet containing the guidelines that all road users – motorists, cyclists and pedestrians – are supposed to be familiar with. Although probably not an ideal state of affairs, the reality is that most people read it before taking a driving test and then don't ever refer to it again.

Drivers are familiar with the penalty system: certain road traffic offences can incur not just fines, imprisonment and driving bans, but various numbers of penalty points, which, when they accumulate after numerous offences, can tip you over the edge into a ban. But if it turns out that the Highway Code is not legally enforceable, maybe we can all happily stop for a picnic on the hard shoulder after all.

It's actually true: the Highway Code is not legally enforceable, because it is a set of guidelines rather than a legislative document. So the Highway Code does not set out 'the law'.

As indicated in the Highway Code itself, many of the guidelines are summarised regulations that are backed up by the law, whether it's wide-reaching legislation like the Road Traffic Act 1991 or specific rules like the Zebra, Pelican and Puffin Pedestrian Crossings Regulations and General Directions 1997 (which presumably does not cover the much-maligned toucan crossings). Other parts of the Highway Code do not have any corresponding laws, but as the Code itself puts it, they 'may be used in evidence in any court proceedings under Traffic Acts to establish liability'.

VERDICT: TRUE

The first edition of the Highway Code, from 1931, rather philosophically entreats the reader to 'bear in mind the difficulties of others and try not to add to them'.

In Switzerland it's illegal to flush the toilet after 10 p.m.

THIS IS A FACT YOU'LL SEE from time to time accompanying news stories in which something 'a bit crazy' happens in Switzerland, in the same way that 'wacky' stories about France will have a sidebar pointing out the Orwellian-sounding restriction that 'no pig may be addressed as Napoleon by its owner'. Indeed, it's almost as if there were an amusing website (hypothetically, let's imagine it could be found at www.dumblaws.com) that lazy journalists referred to every time they wanted to illustrate the 'zaniness' of a country's culture, by copying and pasting some supposedly barmy 'law' that was actually submitted by a random member of the public for a laugh (with the website itself careful to point out that all content is for amusement purposes only).

But of course this isn't actually true: journalists would never be so lazy as to simply copy and paste something from a website and pass it off as fact, since they would much rather spend their time researching information and generating original copy than knock off early and head down the pub for a five-pint lunch.

Despite all this, the Swiss toilet-flushing claim is not completely unfounded: it has its origins in some pretty draconian regulations that you typically have to agree to if you live in an apartment block. Whole blocks tend to be managed by a single agency, with the 'house rules' often posted somewhere prominent – these often feature the 10 p.m. flushing rule as well as very specific variants, such as blokes not urinating while standing up between 10 p.m. and 6 a.m., and fiendish restrictions on the use of washing machines. Of course, all of the above are related to noise pollution rather than some belief in the efficient regulation of toilet use for a healthy society. Defiance of the regulations, which tend to get stricter in the German-speaking parts of the country, is not illegal but you're likely to get chucked out by the management if you're caught having a midnight flush.

VERDICT: FALSE

Switzerland's distinctive square flag (the only square national flag apart from the Vatican's) has to be rectangular when flown at sea, and it used to be triangular.

It's illegal to urinate in a public place, unless you shout the phrase 'In pain!' three times

RESTRICTING THIS TO the UK (for the sake of saving a lifetime of searching every piece of legislation in the world), this is sometimes claimed to apply to the whole country, sometimes only the London Borough of Westminster and sometimes the city of Cardiff. These wild differences in jurisdiction immediately suggest that it is probably utter, if entertaining, nonsense.

The reasoning behind the supposed loophole is that the law provides a curiously defined exception for people who have to urinate in public because they are in physical distress. However, there are no specific laws on the subject of urination.

According to the UK Government's comma-averse 'Cleaner Safer Greener Communities' initiative, ways to combat 'street fouling' include the use of the Public Order Act 1986, the Town

Police Clauses Act 1847 (indecent exposure) and on-the-spot penalties for 'disorderly behaviour', authorised by the Criminal Justice and Police Act 2001. However, by far the most common way that local authorities tackle the issue – in word if not in deed – is by creating a by-law along the lines of: 'No person shall urinate or defecate in any public place.' Westminster Council have done so, but they address the widespread problem in Soho through the intriguing use of portable 'pissoirs' deployed at weekends, rather than through mass arrests.

By-laws are made at the local level, so for any given geographical area a council technically *could* include all sorts of exceptions relating to physical distress or (another common claim) taxi drivers 'urinating on the rear wheel as long as the right hand is touching the vehicle'. Yet, strangely, no written documentation of this seems to exist anywhere.

VERDICT: THROWN OUT DUE TO LACK OF EVIDENCE
Who makes this stuff up?

You can get lottery grants for building work

THIS IS ONE OF MANY SUCH pub facts that are true simply because they are so vague.

The UK's National Lottery was set up in 1994 with the stated purpose of funding 'good causes' – a phrase carefully chosen so as to allow potentially anything to be a recipient if its case could be sufficiently well argued. According to Camelot, who hold the National Lottery Commission licence, 28p from the sale of every

£1 ticket goes towards the 'good causes', with the overall areas benefiting in 2005 being Health, Education, Environment, Community & Charity (50 per cent); Sports (16.67 per cent); Arts (16.67 per cent); and Heritage (16.67 per cent).

Grants awarded range from the parochial (e.g. £2,300 for 'A Project To Increase Participation In The Arts Through The Staging Of A Production Of Macbeth In A Local Church Within The Bridgnorth Area' — what the heck, they might as well have just owned up to which church it was) to the universal (e.g. £31.9 million to build the National Space Centre in Leicester). Probably the highest-profile project funded to date has been the Dome, which during its construction phase surely counted as 'building work'. (Note: the phrase 'Millennium Dome' has now been air-brushed from history.)

The Heritage Lottery Fund, one of several grant-awarding bodies, is the most likely to pay for projects relating to the maintenance of buildings, but if your building serves a community, other options are available. In 2005 for example, the Ashkirk Village Hall Committee, in the Scottish Borders, was awarded £500 via the Community Fund for 'building and labour costs' relating to, er, Ashkirk Village Hall.

As to whether any member of the public can get the National Lottery to cough up for a new conservatory or an extra bedroom above the garage, the chances are quite slim unless you can prove that it will be used as an 'outreach centre' for one morning a week.

VERDICT: SORT OF
One can, but *you* probably *can't.*

Brown sauce is legally allowed to be up to 20 per cent maggots

BROWN SAUCE – denoting a tangy condiment made from vinegar, tomatoes, dates, tamarinds and spices – is a peculiarly British invention. The most recognised brand is HP Sauce, which has many fans in other countries, but it's really only in the UK that people ask for 'brown sauce' (as distinct from 'red sauce', tomato ketchup) without feeling embarrassed. Nevertheless, for seven years the quintessentially British HP Sauce was owned by French food conglomerate Danone.

First properly marketed in 1903 by Edward Samson Moore of the Midland Vinegar Company, HP Sauce was created by a Nottingham grocer, F.G. Garton, who apparently believed that his sauce had been sighted in the Houses of Parliament – although this association became more official when Harold Wilson was (only just) elected prime minister in 1964, as his wife Mary complained in an interview that he drowned everything in HP Sauce.

Wilson would have been shocked to discover that, legally speaking, he might have been smearing maggots all over his lamb chops, bacon sarnies, apple crumbles, fruit salads and lemon sorbets (come on, she did say 'everything'). Needless to say, this is a wholly unfounded claim and no publicly available brown sauce has ever contained maggots, either drowned in vinegar or still squirming.

In theory, with the proper product labelling, there's nothing to stop you selling a brown sauce with as much dead-maggot content as you want, since whatever pub lawyers tell you, there is no legislation relating to the proportion of maggot quantities in vinegar-and-fruit-based table relishes. Selling brown sauce laced with live maggots might, however, lead to a visit from condiment cops when they hear reports of customers squeezing out swarms of sticky flies into cafés up and down the country.

VERDICT: FALSE

A bottle of HP Sauce appears somewhat improbably in a movie version of 1930s America in the 2002 Tom Hanks vehicle *The Road to Perdition*.

In Italy it's illegal to leave a restaurant without taking the receipt with you

DON'T MESS WITH the Guardia di Finanza. When it comes to over-the-top enforcement of paper-pushing, Italy's finance police put on a clinic. If they can spare time away from chasing up Pavarotti's tax returns, they'll stake out eating establishments across the country, waiting to pounce on any departing customers who look like the sort of person who would leave without a receipt.

The reason for this legal curiosity is not because diners in Italy are overly prone to doing runners, but to combat tax evasion. For years it was believed that Italy's restaurateurs were pretty much exclusively doing dodgy cash-in-hand deals, and hence vastly under-reporting their earnings to avoid paying taxes. Therefore, the law requires that as a customer, you must be given a receipt ('*scontrino*') or a more officious invoice ('*ricevuta fiscale*') and keep it on your person when you leave, acting as proof of the transaction.

If you don't get a receipt or you scrunched it up and chucked it in an ashtray on the way out, the implication is that you are colluding in tax avoidance, and Receipt Academy graduates could fine you up to €155.

This doesn't just apply to restaurants but also to most other transactions for goods and services, such as clothes shopping and on-the-spot traffic fines. In fact, if you do get your collar felt by audit-trail cops, when they issue you with the fine it's presumably another test to see whether you ask them for a receipt for paying the penalty – if you don't, they probably keep fining you over and over again on the spot until you finally ask for a receipt. At which point you get banged up for wasting police time.

VERDICT: TRUE

In 1992 a mother was busted to the tune of 33,000 lire (about €25 in today's money) after leaving a shop without a receipt for a 500 lire (€0.35) chocolate bar bought for her two-year-old son.

You're not allowed to smile for your passport photo

WHILE AN EAR-TO-EAR SHIT-EATING GRIN may once have been acceptable for some countries' passports, times have changed, and a sterner view is now taken by most passport-issuing authorities. Since 12 September 2005 the UK Passport Service (UKPS) has been enforcing the strict guidelines drawn up by the International Civil Aviation Organization to enable the use of face-recognition technology at immigration controls, in conjunction with machine-readable passports and other security precautions. And it's not just the UK: all countries within the US Visa Waiver Program have to issue passports containing 'facial biometrics', as do EU signatories to the Schengen Agreement.

Among the more guessable decrees, such as 'the photo should show a close-up of the applicant's head and shoulders', there is a pretty straight-faced explanation of how you should look: the image must show the applicant's 'full face, looking straight at the camera, with a neutral expression, with their mouth closed'. So not only may you not smile but you may not frown, pout, smirk, gurn or grimace, let alone look wistful, quizzical or enigmatic.

The guidelines also specify that the photograph 'should be taken against an off-white, cream or light grey plain background so that the applicant's features are clearly distinguishable against the background.' This explains why photographees of a certain age may exhibit a non-permitted expression of sadness when contemplating the modern-day lack of background curtains, which used to offer a choice of two colours: filthy orange and filthy blue.

VERDICT: TRUE

The UKPS mission is: 'Confirming nationality and identity, enabling travel, by focusing on: Quality, integrity and security;

Excellence in customer service; Developing and motivating staff; Efficiency and value for money; Innovation and improvement' – and maybe issuing passports, too, but only after they've got the other bits sorted out.

If a shop mistakenly advertises something at the wrong price, they have to sell it to you for that amount, because by making an offer they are technically entering into a contract with you

IF THIS IS TRUE the implications of a missing decimal point, a torn price tag or a misprinted billboard are potentially enormous. But surely if advertising something at a price constitutes 'technically entering into a contract with you', it would work both ways: merely by walking into a shop and glancing at a promotional offer you could be legally bound to buy a paper clip for a kajillion dollars.

By advertising or sticking a price tag on something, a shop is not 'technically entering into a contract with you'. In fact, they're not even making you an offer of sale. Technically, they are making what's known as an 'invitation to treat'. Yes, that's right: legalese for 'come on, treat yourself, special price for you, my friend'. This in turn entitles the prospective customer to make them an offer – which they *can* refuse. So if the shop discovers they've been mistakenly advertising a remote-controlled hot tub for the price of a pack of toilet roll, they can simply decide not to sell it. However, if they deliberately displayed ridiculously low prices in order to lure people into their shop, they could potentially be prosecuted under consumer protection laws.

This basically makes common sense, wherever you live – in the US, the legal terminology is 'invitation to bargain' – but before you recount the story of how some website was forced to sell your Aunt Patricia a helicopter for 20 cents due to a software error, it's possible that if the credit card transaction goes through before the mistake is spotted, the helicopter is hers to keep.

VERDICT: FALSE

In 2004 an English rock group from West Yorkshire called Invitation to Treat, with a line-up including two trainee lawyers, recorded a demo titled *Rough Justice* – sadly, they seem to have disbanded and are probably now busy suing each other.

It's not possible to copyright a drum beat

COPYRIGHT IN AN original musical work exists as soon as that work is written down or recorded. (Copyright doesn't exist in ideas: you can't just say, 'I thought of it first.') Copyright is infringed if that work is copied, distributed, performed, broadcast or adapted without the permission of the copyright owner. Simple as that – but what about sampling? Since the birth of hip-hop, a key aspect of many songs is the innovative use of bass lines, breaks, loops and riffs from other recordings. In addition to the song itself copyright also exists in a particular *recording* of that work; copyright in the sound recording is usually owned by the record label rather than the songwriter or the music publisher.

In the early days it was practically illegal *not* to sample James Brown's 'Funky Drummer' or Chic's 'Good Times'. Musicians could sample at will without fear of litigation – not because it was actually legal but because the record companies were too stupid to cash in. They soon wised up and nowadays the threat of legal action is real. Pub lawyers will claim that it's okay 'as long as it's less than eight bars long', or that 'you have to sample more than four notes' – but this is completely false, and sampling just one drum beat technically constitutes infringement. However, a single drum beat on its own is unlikely to be sufficiently recognisable.

So you can infringe copyright by sampling a drum beat that forms part of a larger song – but can you actually 'copyright a drum beat', by recording a single drum beat and giving it a title like 'She Bangs the Drum'? There is no definition of 'music' in the UK's Copyright, Designs and Patents Act 1988 or similar legislation in other countries, which means that in a legal context you would be able to draw on dictionary definitions and expert musicologists. These would probably require your 'song' to exhibit at least one of either harmony, melody or rhythm, so you'd be laughed out of court.

VERDICT: IMPRACTICAL

In the 1990s it was rumoured that Polygram (which later became part of Universal) set up an entire department whose sole function was to listen to records and check for unlicensed James Brown samples – unfortunately, evidence for this being true is sketchy at best.

You can't libel dead people

IN GENERAL TERMS, libel is the publication of a defamatory statement about an identifiable person or corporation, where 'defamatory' basically means 'likely to significantly damage that person or corporation's reputation in the eyes of society'. This is not to be confused with slander – which is a spoken or transient defamatory statement – and the person or institution does not need to be named in order to be 'identifiable'. For example, making a defamatory statement about 'that food company with the Golden Arches logo' could land you in hot water – or hot oil, at least.

The exact mechanics, of course, vary across legal systems. For example, US libel laws tend to favour the defendant, whereas under English law the plaintiff tends to have an easier time of it because the burden of proof is on the publisher of the statement. In both the US and the UK, however, no one (not the family, heirs, friends, business partners or others) can sue for libel on behalf of a dead person. This means you can speak as ill as you like of the dead, because the dead person no longer has a reputation to maintain.

You could, however, potentially have some sort of claim if you can show that the libellous statement against the dead person implies libel against yourself, or if you have incurred financial losses as a result of a defamatory statement against a dead person – for example, if you inherited a fast-food business from your father, about whom it was then falsely written that he had a hereditary obsessive-compulsive disorder that caused him repeatedly to deep-fry rats instead of chickens.

VERDICT: TRUE
Ronald Reagan used to regularly indulge in depraved sex games
with Dame Thora Hird in the Oval Office.

It's illegal to burn money

YOU'LL HEAR MANY versions of this: it's illegal to burn or
deface money; it's not illegal to deface money, but it *is* illegal to
use money that has been defaced; and so on. Obviously it depends
where you live, but in the UK burning money – while it is
incredibly stupid – is *not* illegal. Defacing money, on the other
hand, *is* subject to a penalty as per the Currency and Bank Notes
Act 1928.

The reasoning behind this discrepancy, or the lack of any need
to prohibit money-burning, seems to be that you could attempt to
keep a defaced note in circulation, whereas once your stash has
gone up in smoke it's gone for ever – so you've simply removed
your currency from the system. (If you try to burn someone else's
money, other laws will swiftly kick in.)

Notes do get mutilated, defaced and destroyed, of course. The
average lifespan of a £5 note is only around one year, according to
the Bank of England, who also allow you to send off mutilated
notes and apply for replacements via their cash centre in Leeds. In
2004 alone, claims were made for 4,272 'chewed or eaten' notes to
the value of £86,000. The Bank itself no longer burns used notes,
preferring to shred them (though some shreddings end up in
commercial incinerators).

In 1994 professional timewasters The K Foundation (previously known as the KLF, among other incarnations) burned a million pounds and got away with it. But they had previously been fined £9,000, plus £500 'reprint costs', for defacing a million pounds' worth of £50 notes by nailing them to an art gallery wall.

VERDICT: FALSE IN THE UK

Burning money is illegal (and punishable by a five-year prison sentence) in India, where there were calls for the arrest of politician K. Keshav Rao in 2006 after he performed a magic trick where he appeared to burn a 100-rupee note.

Computer games are illegal in Greece

IT'S DIFFICULT TO BELIEVE that in the birthplace of Western civilisation it's illegal to play *Sid Meier's Civilization*; and that a country known for inventing the Olympic Games could be humourless enough to ban *Daley Thompson's Decathlon*. Yet that's exactly what the party-pooping Greek authorities did when they introduced law 3037, effective from July 2002, which banned all computer and video games. That's *all* electronic games, be it a coin-operated *Pac-Man* machine, *Snake* on your mobile phone, *PONG* on your TV, *Tetris* on a hand-held console, a fruit machine, those poker machines that don't even pay out, *Quake*, *Tomb Raider*, *Horace Goes Skiing* or *Super Mario Anything*. Not even *Minesweeper*, which you never knew you'd installed in the first place. Nothing, whether in the street, in an Internet café or in your own home.

In case you presumed that this was merely a ridiculous technicality that would never actually be enforced, think on. In the first

six months of 2004 the authorities said that they had conducted over a thousand raids – and with penalties ranging from a minimum of three months in jail plus a €5,000 fine, to a maximum of one year in jail plus a €75,000 fine for repeat offenders, opposition to the law has been fierce. In one of the first prosecution attempts in 2002, against a cybercafé flagrantly allowing customers to play *Counter-Strike* and online chess, the court hearing the case determined that the law was unconstitutional.

Pressure from the public and the EU led to a clarification of the law so that it only applied to Internet cafés and gambling games, but by 2005 Greece had been referred to the European Court of Justice, primarily because the ban contravenes the principle of the free movement of goods from other EU member states – and *because it's frickin' stupid*. The Greek authorities have eased off for the time being, but the law has not yet actually been repealed.

VERDICT: TRUE

The original reason for the law was to crack down on Greece's huge problem of illegal gambling, highlighted when Alekos Chrisanthakopoulos, an MP who chaired a parliamentary committee on gambling, was caught on camera playing an illegal one-armed bandit.

You can be fined £30 for having an italics number plate

BY THE END OF THE twentieth century, Britain was running out of numbers for vehicle licensing, so the system was changed in 2001 to accommodate a new registration format. While they were at it they also made some changes to the way registration should be displayed on new vehicles – in other words, changes to the physical number plates themselves (known in the US as 'license plates'). Some of the changes are to prevent conflicts with European standards, while others relate to police work (marking plates for subsequent tracing and computer recognition of registration numbers via camera).

There are some extraordinarily specific rules laid out in the succinctly titled Road Vehicles (Display of Registration Marks) Regulations 2001, with one of the key introductions being the mandatory use of the all-capitals 'prescribed font'. The font is reproduced in Schedule 4 of the regulations, in the only two permitted character heights (79 millimetres and 64 millimetres). Use of an italic script or 'a font, other than italic script, in which the characters are not vertical' is strictly forbidden. You could in fact be subject to a maximum fine of £1,000 – but from offences reported to date it seems that you're more likely to get a £30 fixed-penalty ticket, unless perhaps you are a persistent font felon.

Although the 'prescribed font' is the norm, technically, with a few other exceptions, you may legally display a number plate in a font that is 'substantially similar'. Hardcore typography fans will be delighted to learn that the law specifically states that both serif and sans serif fonts are permissible, providing all the other conditions are met. Whatever font you use, it won't make the grammatically bungled phrase 'an italics number plate' any more acceptable.

VERDICT: TRUE

Don't even *think* about getting a number plate made up using Wingdings.

It's illegal to get divorced in Malta

THERE'S A REASON WHY Steely Dan wrote a song called 'Haitian Divorce' and not 'Maltese Divorce'. (There's also a reason why Dashiell Hammett wrote a book called *The Maltese Falcon* and not *The Haitian Falcon*, but that's a different reason.) In other words, if you're looking for a 'quickie' divorce, you'd be advised to give the island of Malta a wide berth – otherwise, you'll be waiting a very long time.

Following Chile's introduction of relevant legislation in 2004, seven years after the Republic of Ireland, it seems that Malta and the Philippines – both also predominantly Catholic societies – are the only two remaining countries in the world that don't have divorce laws. Note that the notion of 'not being able to get a divorce because there is no divorce law' is not the same thing as 'it's illegal to get divorced'; but in the world of the pub lawyer (who's too busy setting the world to rights to be worried by the tiresome notion of accuracy) the phrase 'it's illegal' is simply the formal – and hence more believable – version of 'you can't'. To put it another way, it's not as if you and your spouse could sneak down to a backstreet judge and then get busted by the wedding police halfway through the hearing: you simply can't get divorced.

From a religious point of view, the Catholic Church does, in general, provide for the notion of annulment (for example, declaring a union to be void because the person you married turned out to be a gorilla wearing a human suit), but Malta does not provide any legal framework for divorce. You can obtain a legal 'separation', which takes care of the administrative aspects of property and child custody – but separated couples may not remarry since they remain married to each other. Membership of the European Union, achieved in 2004, has not made any difference, except to bind Malta legally to recognise divorces made in other countries – something which Malta previously did anyway.

In 2004 the media-hungry lawyer Emmy Bezzina set up Malta's pro-divorce Alpha Liberal Democratic Reformist Party, with the slogan 'one belief, one team, one focus' – which sounds like a lost verse from 'One Vision' by Queen. Alpha has not proved especially popular with the electorate.

VERDICT: BASICALLY TRUE

Hollywood legend Zsa Zsa Gabor is no stranger to the legal complexities of marriage: in 1977 she married Michael O'Hara, her divorce lawyer from her sixth marriage – and five years later she bigamously married Felipe de Alba, a union that she had to get annulled.

History

The parachute was invented before the aeroplane

WHILE THE PARACHUTE is naturally associated with jumping from planes, it's not so surprising that a means to slow a person's descent through the air came first: hot-air balloon passengers may have needed some form of safety apparatus, and well before that there were blokes desperate to prove how brave they were by pointlessly jumping off tall buildings. Some things never change.

The first such idiot may have been Armen Firman, who jumped from a tower in the Spanish city of Córdoba in AD 852, using a cloak with wooden struts. His intention was to fly, or at least glide, but the cloak turned out to be just a survival mechanism.

A parachute sketch appears in Leonardo da Vinci's *Codex Atlanticus*. In a sweeping, pub fact generalisation, he wrote that with the necessary design 'anyone could jump from any height whatsoever without any risk'. His parachute – linen stretched over a pyramid-shaped frame of wooden poles – was tested 'successfully' in 2000 by bone-headed skydiver Adrian Nicholas. But even he wimped out mid-fall and switched to a modern parachute, scared of being killed on landing by the weight of the frame.

The first person deliberately to jump using a parachute (and survive) was Louis-Sébastien Lenormand in 1783. By the 1790s parachutes were being made from silk, with other Frenchmen such as André-Jacques Garnerin and Jean-Pierre Blanchard jumping from balloons; the French word *parachute* ('protection from falling') dates from this time. In 1912 US Army Captain Albert Berry became the first person to parachute from an aeroplane.

VERDICT: TRUE

The invention of the aeroplane is credited to the Wright brothers because their 1903 contraption could reliably repeat flights over practical distances, although short self-propelled flights were undertaken by Clément Ader in the 1890s, and George Cayley completed the first manned glider flight in 1853.

Dante Gabriel Rossetti had a pet wombat

THE CO-FOUNDER of the Pre-Raphaelite brotherhood (which to modern ears sounds like an LA street gang) was a big fan of exotic animals, and built up a substantial menagerie at his house in Cheyne Walk, Chelsea. As well as the wombat bought in 1869, which Rossetti described as 'a joy, a triumph, a delight, a madness', we know from his brother's memoirs that he kept armadillos, jackasses, wallabies, a racoon, salamanders, chameleons, kangaroos, and many other animals.

Everyone connected with the Pre-Raphaelite movement was

obsessed with wombats. Edward Burne-Jones used to sketch them regularly and helped Rossetti and others redecorate the Oxford Union with lots of wombat scenes in 1857. Christina Rossetti wrote the Italian poem 'O Uommibatto' ('O Wombat') on first seeing her brother's new pet, and in her verse fairy-tale *Goblin Market*, written seven years earlier, she compared one of the goblins to the 'obtuse and furry' Australian marsupial.

Dante Gabriel Rossetti bestowed his wombat with special significance when he made a ham-fisted sketch of the object of his infatuation, Jane Morris, holding the animal on a leash – seemingly representing her husband William. And he named the wombat Top, surely after William's nickname 'Topsy'.

Sadly, Top died within two months of moving in – not after eating a box of cigars, as claimed by the American artist Whistler – and Rossetti wasted no time in getting Top stuffed. There was briefly a second wombat, which died even sooner after its arrival, but Rossetti appears to have transferred his affections onto a woodchuck.

VERDICT: TRUE

It is sometimes suggested that Rossetti's friend Lewis Carroll used the wombat as the inspiration for the dormouse in *Alice's Adventures in Wonderland*, but this was written several years before the purchase of Top; it may be significant, however, that Rossetti also kept dormice at Cheyne Walk.

The DustBuster was invented by NASA

YOU KNOW THE DUSTBUSTER – that convenient, hand-held cleaning device for those hard-to-reach areas? It's a registered trademark of Black & Decker; so did Black & Decker steal or licence the technology from the American space agency? And are NASA's astronauts really so untidy that they had to invent their own vacuum cleaner?

Needless to say, the truth is out there, somewhere. For the Apollo programme – which led to the moon landings and that awful Tom Hanks film – NASA boffins realised that they would need a drill for collecting moon rock samples that had to be light-weight and hand-held. So in the 1960s they teamed up with power tool manufacturers Black & Decker to develop something suitable.

The key innovation, according to NASA, was the use of a computer program to 'design the drill's motor to use as little power as possible'. This computer program and the surrounding research,

which created the Apollo Lunar Surface Drill, was subsequently used by Black & Decker for a whole range of hand-held appliances, including the DustBuster. So it's not true that NASA invented the DustBuster specifically; they simply had a hand in the technology that made it and other battery-powered tools possible.

Suppose, though, that NASA had invented the DustBuster for

collecting lunar granules or space dust. They'd have been pretty irritated to discover that a vacuum cleaner would have no effect up there, since outer space is itself a vacuum – so there would be no means to create suction using the tool.

VERDICT: FALSE, BUT ONLY JUST

NASA runs a technology transfer division, whose objective is to help develop the commercial application of technologies designed for space use, such as CAT scanning, smoke detectors and, er, ribbed swimsuits.

Coca-Cola used to contain cocaine

As one of the world's most recognised and purchased brands, Coca-Cola has become the subject of countless urban myths and spurious allegations. Invented by a pharmacist, John Pemberton, it first went on sale in 1886 as a medicine that, according to Pemberton, cured headaches, impotence and morphine addiction. Clearly he failed to take a taste of his own medicine as he was a morphine addict himself when he sold the rights to two different businesses. Pemberton's son Charley (who later died of an opium overdose) was a shareholder in one of these businesses, but fell out with the other owners and started selling his own version of the drink.

The Coca-Cola Corporation that exists today was founded in 1892 by Asa Griggs Candler (who initially tried marketing his version of the drink as Yum Yum and then Koke) in an attempt to control the market – an attempt that was successful and highly lucrative, although shrouded in claims of forged signatures, burning of paperwork and the sorts of business practices that make Enron's behaviour in the 1990s look like a model of corporate governance.

So what was in the stuff? One of Coca-Cola's most successful marketing strategies has been to promote an aura of intense secrecy around the drink's formula, with the identity of one ingredient in particular, the so-called 7X, purported to be kept in a high-security vault in Atlanta, Georgia. However, one thing is clear: the drink took its name from two of its many ingredients, coca leaf and kola nut. The cocaine content derived from the extract of coca leaf. When the drink was invented, cocaine was still regarded as something of a wonder drug, like heroin (see p. 137) – but as public concern grew, Coke's makers eventually eliminated the use of coca extract, favouring spent coca leaves (the residue after cocaine extraction) rather than cocaine itself.

VERDICT: TRUE

If you reckon the original coke-based Coke would give you a buzz, imagine Pemberton's previous version of the drink, created before Atlanta banned booze in 1885, which was a 'coca wine': a mind-bending cocktail of alcohol, caffeine and cocaine.

Casanova invented the national lottery

GIACOMO CASANOVA, the eighteenth-century adventurer, writer and ladies' man, is sometimes claimed to have invented the concept of the state lottery, setting up the first such enterprise in

France in the late 1750s – a lottery that Claude Monet supposedly went on to win (see p. 213).

According to Professor Stephen Stigler of the University of Chicago, the lottery that Casanova is said to have 'invented' was in fact neither the first of its kind nor the brainchild of Casanova. He was, however, instrumental in using his influence and seductive sales techniques to promote the idea enthusiastically to a sceptical Louis XV, to help finance the completion of the *Ecole militaire*.

In the West the lottery as we know it (betting money on randomly selected numbers) seems to have been invented by a Genoan businessman in 1626, inspired by the city-state's system of drawing lots to decide which five noblemen would serve on the council. Casanova would have been familiar with this before being imprisoned in Venice for witchcraft and then escaping to Paris. Other forms of lottery, such as the 'blanks lottery', which today we would probably term a 'raffle', were well known before Casanova's time – in France and elsewhere, sanctioned by the state. As with most inventions, the Chinese beat the rest of the world to it, with lottery games appearing during the Han dynasty.

VERDICT: STATISTICALLY FALSE

In 1728, in an earlier form of lottery, the writer and philosopher Voltaire (whom Casanova later met) was part of a syndicate that got rich by buying up all the tickets – after the French government mistakenly authorised a system in which the overall prize money was significantly more than the total cost of the tickets. D'oh!

Russians celebrate the October Revolution in November

THE RUSSIAN REVOLUTION OF 1917, which replaced the monarchy with a Communist state, was not an instantaneous process, though there were a number of distinct events during the course of the year that marked dramatic change. The two key phases were the February Revolution, which led to the abdication of Tsar Nicholas II, and the October Revolution, in which Alexander Kerensky's provisional government was overthrown by the Bolsheviks under the leadership of Lenin and Trotsky.

The October Uprising, as it was initially known (later officially re-branded as the Great October Socialist Revolution), did literally signal an overnight change. It started on 25 October and ended with the taking of St Petersburg's Winter Palace in the early hours of the following morning. Hence the October bit.

Its anniversary is marked (if not 'celebrated') in November because, at the time, Russia was using a different date system, the Julian calendar ('old style' dates), to the current one, the Gregorian calendar ('new style' dates). The Gregorian calendar was officially adopted by Russia in 1918 when 1 February 1918 (old style) became 14 February 1918 (new style). Thus, what *was* 25 October is nowadays 7 November – but even when the revolution was taking place, the date was confusing, since by 1917 most other countries in the world had already adopted the Gregorian calendar. And, yes, that means the February Revolution happened in March.

VERDICT: TRUE

Most of Munich's Oktoberfest takes place in September.

Shakespeare invented the word 'alligator'

IT IS RARE TO BE able to pinpoint a single person as the 'inventor' of an English word this old, especially when it describes something from the natural world like an animal or plant. And like so much of modern-day English, 'alligator' can be easily traced to the corruption of a word borrowed from another language – in this case, the Spanish *el lagarto*, meaning 'the lizard'.

Shakespeare, innovative though he may have been, wasn't the first person to write down the word in English. Before the Bard, the *Oxford English Dictionary* cites four usages of the word, variously 'lagarto', 'aligarto' and 'alagarto', starting with Job Hortop, who wrote of 'a monstrous Lagarto or Crocodile' in 1568 (when Shakespeare was four years old). Shakespeare's first written reference to the 'aligarta' was in a 1597 quarto edition of *Romeo and Juliet*, with the spelling later changed to 'allegater' in 1623's posthumous First Folio. (He probably wouldn't have lost any sleep over this, as a man who wasn't even sure how to spell his own surname.)

So the correct version of this fact might be: 'Shakespeare was the first writer in the English language to be attributed (posthumously) the use of a form ending in "-r" for the word whose spelling has now been standardised as "alligator".' Hardly going to impress your friends down the pub, is it?

VERDICT: AN HEDGE-BORN GALLIMAUFRY OF CAUTELOUS BAVIN

Shakespeare did invent the word 'puke', or rather 'puking', which makes its first appearance in the English language in Jaques' 'All the world's a stage' speech from *As You Like It*.

John F. Kennedy had a really bad back

HISTORIANS AREN'T CONCERNED about such trivia as the Cuban Missile Crisis, the Berlin Wall or grassy knolls: what JFK will surely be remembered for is having a really bad back.

In fact the subject of JFK's health has been regarded as historically significant – his 1960 presidential win relied heavily on the image of a youthful, healthy antidote to the creaky old Eisenhower regime. As revealed by the historian Robert Dallek, who was the first to be granted access to long-secret medical files during the research for his book *An Unfinished Life: John F. Kennedy 1917–1963*, there was a major cover-up in place to prevent the voting public from realising the extent of JFK's health problems.

From childhood John F. Kennedy suffered a truly bewildering array of afflictions, including measles, chicken pox, jaundice, whooping cough, diphtheria, scarlet fever, bronchitis, malaria, Addison's disease, an unspecified thyroid condition, irritable bowel syndrome, osteoporosis, colitis, high cholesterol and migraines. By the end of his life he was popping more pills than Elvis, and was being pumped full of steroids and other medications. During his first summit with Nikita Khrushchev, one of his physicians, Max 'Dr Feelgood' Jacobson, was even giving the president amphetamine shots. Rock 'n' roll!

On top of all this he suffered from chronic back pain, due to an injury incurred while he was in command of a PT (patrol torpedo) boat near the Solomon Islands during the Second World War. (This incident boosted his 'war hero' status, and was later turned into a book and a film, *PT 109*.) He repeatedly needed surgery on his back, and required frequent injections of novocaine.

You might think that a bad back pales into insignificance alongside JFK's full house of other medical ailments, but one of the many theories surrounding his assassination is that the back brace he was wearing that day in Dallas prevented his body falling forward after the first bullet, a movement that would have caused the second bullet to miss, thereby saving his life.

VERDICT: TRUE

JFK received the last rites on at least three occasions, and never fully overcame the stigma of being named after an airport.

The Empire State Building was originally built as a disembarkation point for Nazi hot-air balloons

THE EMPIRE STATE BUILDING OPENED in 1931. In Germany the Nazi Party came to power two years later, although they had been growing in influence for over a decade. After 1933, German Zeppelins adorned with the Nazi swastika were visitors to the New York skyline, but there was no such thing as a 'Nazi hot-air balloon' when the Empire State Building was constructed. Yet buried behind the preposterous historical confusion of this claim lurks a certain half-truth.

The iconic landmark was originally designed to have a flat roof, but financier John J. Raskob decided that it needed a 'hat'. Like many at the time, he was convinced that dirigible airships (otherwise known as blimps or, in pub terminology, 'hot-air balloons') represented the future of aviation. So he had an 'airship station' added to the top, amid great publicity.

The building was equipped with a mooring mast, a departure lounge and docking machinery, as well as a narrow walkway onto the mast. In reality, however, because an airship could only be tethered from its nose, keeping a craft stable enough for dis-embarkation proved utterly impractical. Passengers probably wouldn't have been keen on the whole 'windy gangway and steep ladders' concept either – but they didn't get a chance to try.

Only one small craft ever managed to dock during testing, and then only for three minutes; photographs showing huge airships moored to the building are 'artist's impression' composites designed for advertising purposes. Nowadays the departure lounge serves as the building's observation deck and gift shop.

VERDICT: FALSE

The turgid 2004 film *Sky Captain and the World of Tomorrow* re-creates how the scene might have looked.

Pope Benedict XVI was in the Hitler Youth

WHEN CARDINAL JOSEPH RATZINGER WAS elected Pope Benedict XVI in April 2005, his upbringing in Germany prompted a media frenzy, with suggestions that the new leader was somehow mired in a shadowy extremist past and was not best placed to lead the Catholic Church. The fact that he was already regarded as a conservative didn't encourage the image of a warm and fluffy 'go-to guy' for spiritual guidance: nicknamed God's Rottweiler, he once denounced rock music as 'the vehicle of anti-religion', which suggests he's never taken time out to listen to the music of Cliff Richard.

As a slight digression, when writing about the Pope, it's obligatory to refer to him in the second paragraph as 'the Pontiff', and then revert to 'the Pope' again afterwards. Now we've got that out of the way, let's get on with the investigation.

Ratzinger was born in Bavaria in 1927, so his formative years were dominated by the rise of the Nazi Party and the Second World War. The Hitler Youth was effectively used as a recruiting organisation for the Nazis, promoting dedication to the Third Reich and the 'ideals' of Aryanism, and by the time the future Pope joined, membership of the movement had become compulsory; any portrayals of Ratzinger as an enthusiastic young supporter of Nazi causes are wholly without basis.

Compared to countless others, the Catholic Ratzinger was relatively lucky. Drafted into a labour battalion in 1944, and then into an anti-aircraft corps, he managed to desert during the last weeks of the war without getting caught, but was then interned by the Americans in a prisoner-of-war camp for six weeks, before being released in June 1945.

VERDICT: TRUE

In 2006 Benedict XVI became the first Pope to own an MP3 player, which was a gift from the employees of Vatican Radio.

The electric chair was invented by a dentist

BEING FORCED TO SIT in a chair and undergo an unpleasant experience is something common to dentistry and electrocution – although perhaps the latter is marginally worse. Thus it's fitting to think that it was a dentist who invented the chair-based execution technology, rather than, for example, an interior designer.

Dentist Dr Alfred Southwick of Buffalo, New York, cooked up the idea of using electricity as a more humane means of execution than hanging (after seeing a drunk die as a result of accidentally touching a generator), although he didn't actually invent the chair itself. Southwick found his way onto a commission investigating 'the most humane and practical method' of executing criminals, whose recommendations led to electrocution replacing hanging in New York State after 1888. (It's tempting to imagine Southwick asking 'Is it safe?' in the manner of *Marathon Man*.)

Not long before this, Thomas 'light bulbs' Edison had developed a DC electricity distribution system, but was losing out commercially to George Westinghouse's more practical AC system, based on the ideas of Nikola Tesla. Edison decided that one way to promote DC as a safer technology for homes and cities was to associate the rival AC system with death, by publicising fatal accidents caused by AC electrocution. An Edison supporter, Harold P. Brown, started a campaign for the banning of AC systems, and publicly electrocuted animals using AC and DC power, intending to demonstrate that AC was lethal (whereas electrocuting animals with DC was no doubt all a bit of harmless fun). Westinghouse was enraged, although he declined to take up Brown's maverick challenge of a duel in which they would both be subjected to electrocution via their favoured types of current.

All this publicity had Edison's desired effect (though he lost out in the long run). Westinghouse's AC system was chosen for the electric chair, and the 'expert' chosen to design the first chair was none other than Harold Brown himself — who had to get hold of Westinghouse equipment on the sly.

VERDICT: FALSE

English footballer Paul Gascoigne popularised the concept of the 'dentist's chair' as an alcohol delivery mechanism.

Americans and Canadians celebrate Thanksgiving in different months

THIS IS, QUITE SIMPLY, TRUE. In the US Thanksgiving is in November, while in Canada it's in October. In the rest of the world Thanksgiving can seem like a mysterious concept whose significance is not always fully understood, though similar celebrations, usually taking harvest as their theme, have long existed in many countries.

Thanksgiving is associated with big family reunions centred around gut-busting festive dinners of turkey, stuffing, cranberry sauce, candied yams and pumpkin pie, although of course there are many regional variations when it comes to traditional dishes. But the meaning behind all the face-filling is to give thanks to God — or nature more generally, if you're not religious — for the food of the land and the fact that, hey, we're all still here and isn't it great?

Historically, the American Thanksgiving is associated with a harvest knees-up held by a group of Pilgrims in 1621 in Plymouth, Massachusetts, in honour of the native Wampanoag people, thanks to whom they had survived the previous winter. (Historians also identify earlier Thanksgiving meals involving Spanish conquistadors.) Numerous Thanksgivings were subsequently held on different dates, with the current timing – the fourth Thursday in November – becoming official in 1941.

In Canada Thanksgiving is traced back to a feast held in Newfoundland by the explorer Sir Martin Frobisher in 1578. Again, dates varied over the years, with some Thanksgiving celebrations dedicated to specific events such as Armistice Day, until 1957, when it was officially set as the second Monday in October – a date when Americans are busy celebrating, or at least debating the political correctness of, Columbus Day.

VERDICT: TRUE

Benjamin Franklin wanted the turkey to be the national bird of the United States instead of the bald eagle.

The concept of teenagers didn't exist until the 1950s

OBVIOUSLY TEENAGERS THEMSELVES have existed for as long as humans have (or technically, perhaps, for thirteen years fewer than humans have), but the idea of teenagers as a distinct socio-cultural group hasn't. The suggestion is that until the 1950s

teenagers were not viewed as an identifiable part
of youth beyond 'adolescence'.

That, really, is where you could argue the case:
at face value 'teenager' literally means a
person whose age ends in '-teen' – so
anyone between thirteen and nine-
teen, an age that approximately
overlaps with adolescence. Yet after
the Second World War, in America
especially, the concept of 'teenagers'
(perhaps simply a more palatable
word than 'adolescents') certainly
became associated in popular culture with
more than just the physical and psychologi-
cal transition between childhood and adulthood. 'Teenagers'
evoked rebellious images of James Dean and a sector of society that
– in contrast to any other time in recent history – suddenly 'had it
so good' that they could buy into rock 'n' roll, drive-in movies and
'Enchantment under the Sea' dance nights.

Without wishing to open up a massive can of semiotic worms,
it's reasonable to say that for a word to denote a concept, it helps
if the word exists. Whilst 'adolescence' and 'adolescent' have been
around since the fifteenth century, 'teenager' is certainly a more
recent addition to the English language, with the *Oxford English
Dictionary*'s earliest citation dated to 1941. The adjective 'teenage'
has been with us a little longer, at least since the 1920s. This
makes it fair to conclude that the 'concept of teenagers' existed, in
some form, prior to the 1950s.

VERDICT: FALSE
Whatever the merits of the words 'teenager' and 'adolescent', there was absolutely no justification for the title of the 2006 Britflick *KiDULTHOOD*.

Technically, North and South Korea are still at war

IF YOU THOUGHT the Korean War ended over 50 years ago, you'd be wrong. That apocryphal American soldier who's still holed up in the jungle somewhere, eating snakes and walking around on tiptoes because he doesn't think the war has ended yet, is *actually right*.

An armistice came into effect on 27 July 1953, signed by Kim Il-Sung (for North Korea), Peng Dehuai (for China) and Mark W. Clark (for the United Nations forces) – but no one from the South Korean side ever bothered signing it. However, the reason that the war has never officially ended is not because the South Koreans had 'dropped their pen' but because no peace treaty was ever negotiated. An armistice is a formal agreement to suspend hostilities – in a less temporary sense than a simple cease-fire – but it needs to be followed by a peace treaty, just like the 1919 Treaty of Versailles followed the armistice signed at the end of the First World War in 1918.

Then again, you could try to argue that the war was never properly started in the first place. For a while, the USA termed it the Korean Conflict, to cover themselves for the fact that while the administration had received international backing in the form of the United Nations, they were effectively fighting as the United States without having obtained a congressional declaration of war.

VERDICT: TRUE

Technically, this means that the cast of M*A*S*H have to be coaxed out of retirement for one last episode.

Tea bags were invented by accident

IT COULD HAPPEN TO ANYONE, really. One minute you fancy a caffeine break, get the pot ready and reach for the tin of loose-leaf tea as the water comes to the boil – and the next minute, you've accidentally divided up the tea into small piles, each of which you've sealed into a bag made of a porous material that will allow the flavour to diffuse without needing to use a tea-strainer or clog up the sink.

This is exactly what didn't happen to New York tea magnate Thomas Sullivan. In 1904 (or 1908 according to some sources) he decided that it would be more cost-effective to send samples to prospective customers in quantities smaller than tins or boxes, and so he started distributing tea in little silk bags that he sewed up by hand. In the style of the person in the Chinese restaurant who mistakenly drinks the contents of the finger-bowl, the recipients thought that Sullivan had deliberately created a dunkable tea-infusion system, and started ordering more of these new-fangled 'tea bags'. As the bags' popularity grew, the material changed from silk to gauze and then paper, and nowadays loose-leaf tea is the rarity compared to the ubiquitous bag.

Similar possibilities existed prior to Sullivan's invention, most notably in the form of metal 'tea eggs' and other infusers, but the pre-filled tea bag basically owes its existence to the bungling recipients of a direct-marketing campaign.

VERDICT: TRUE
John Harvey Kellogg and his brother Will Keith Kellogg accidentally invented cornflakes.

António Salazar was killed by a deckchair

ANTÓNIO DE OLIVEIRA SALAZAR, the Portuguese prime minister and de facto dictator, was 81 years old when he died in Lisbon in 1970, so the idea of a frail old man being folded to death in a collapsible chair might not seem so far-fetched. Or perhaps he was edging slowly along the beachfront, Zimmer-frame first, when a strong gust of wind caused a deckchair to fly through the air and knock him to the ground, stone dead.

The reality is a little less dramatic. In 1968, while staying at his seaside residence in São João do Estoril, Salazar's deckchair collapsed under him, triggering a stroke (something *Time* magazine described at the time as 'a nasty spill'). After an operation to remove a blood clot from his brain, he fell into a life-threatening coma. He made enough of a recovery to leave hospital a few months later, but the lasting brain damage and paralysis left him so severely incapacitated that Portugal's president, Américo Tomás, appointed Marcelo Caetano as the new prime minister.

When Salazar died over a year and a half after the deckchair incident, he was reported to be convinced that he was still prime minister. Some claim that this was because he was delusional; others maintain that everyone was too scared to tell him; and there is also a slightly baffling theory that he knew he was no longer the boss but was just 'playing along'.

VERDICT: GENEROUS WITH THE TRUTH

Nevertheless, it is always prudent to check that the notches have fully engaged before you sit in a deckchair, even if it is on a 'safe' surface such as a sandy beach.

The fax machine was invented in the nineteenth century

IT'S EASY TO THINK OF THE FAX, or facsimile machine, as being 'so 1980s' – as symbolic of that decade as Gordon Gekko, massive shoulder pads and Duran Duran. Like Duran Duran, however, not only was the fax still limping along at the start of the twenty-first century, it was also by then over 150 years old. So old that it actually pre-dates the telephone, which is surprising since modern fax machines use the telephone network.

The father of the fax was Alexander Bain, a Scottish clock-maker who incorporated a pendulum into what he called, after much brainstorming, Bain's Telegraph. By the time he devised and patented his invention in 1843, the electric telegraph had been around for a few years, but the key difference with Bain's Telegraph was its ability to produce remotely an exact copy of physical lines, letters or shapes, rather than simply to transmit a predefined set of

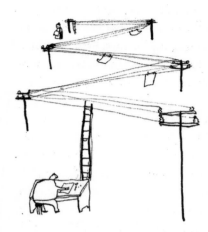

letters or numbers as codes. So Bain became the first person to transmit an image over a wire.

Bain's Telegraph, as you might expect, wasn't quite as flexible as the electronic fax machines or associated digital gizmos that are familiar today. The source image had to be created on a metal sheet, which was scanned using a stylus attached to the pendulum, with the dark and light areas transmitted as electrical impulses and reproduced at the receiving end by another pendulum staining chemically treated paper. The underlying principles of Bain's approach – to scan a document for light and dark areas and transmit the corresponding data – formed the basis for all subsequent fax devices.

VERDICT: TRUE

Oscar-winning actor Daniel Day-Lewis was rumoured to have dumped girlfriend Isabelle Adjani by fax.

The Hundred Years' War lasted 116 years

THE HUNDRED YEARS WAR or the Hundred Years' War? The presence of an apostrophe is a moot point among historians and editors the world over, who use the phrase to refer to what was actually a series of wars between England and France during the fourteenth and fifteenth centuries. The war's 'greatest hits', if you will, include the Battle of Agincourt, the burning of Joan of Arc at the stake, and the Siege of Calais, when thousands of day-trippers from Kent descended upon the local hypermarkets demanding cheap booze.

Although the conflicts could be said to have their roots in earlier centuries, in the sense that Europe has been one big battleground since the year dot, the generally agreed dates for the Hundred Years' War are 1337–1453. So yes, 116 years in total, which is not really that surprising: what history professor wants to go around lecturing about the Hundred and Sixteen Years' War? It takes nearly twice as long to say. A hundred is a nice round figure that imparts the general flavour of the hostilities: they went on for a *very* long time.

The description is, of course, something bestowed retrospectively by historians trying to make sense of the disparate events of the past. It's not as if the war was called the Hundred Years' War when it started out; even the most accomplished of spin doctors would have a hard time selling that one to the people. Although perhaps if they'd managed to do so, and then faced complaints once fighting raged on into the hundred and first year, they could have claimed that the war had now gone into injury time.

VERDICT: TRUE

By the time of the Thirty Years' War (1618–48) and the Seven Years' War (1756–63), history chiefs managed to get their sums right.

The Milky Way used to be called the Fat Emma

TO ANY NORMAL PERSON, the history of the Milky Way represents a confused inability to properly promote chocolate bars. To those who work in marketing, however, it is probably a 'best-practice case study' of how to invoke 'evolving brand management' and successfully 'facilitate increased customer onboarding'.

In the US the bar known by the name of the Milky Way is identical to that sold in the rest of the world as the Mars Bar. This wouldn't be so baffling except that there is also a Milky Way sold in the UK and elsewhere that is a different product.

The American Milky Way was originally created in 1923, with two versions: chocolate and vanilla. The latter was subsequently re-branded as the Forever Yours – a poor choice of name, given that it was discontinued in 1979. However, it reappeared a decade later as the Milky Way Dark bar, and has since been re-re-branded as the Milky Way Midnight.

So where does the charming-sounding Fat Emma fit in? In the 1920s, the Pendergast Candy Company accidentally developed an all-new fluffy nougat recipe that was highly successful and became known as Minnesota (or Minneapolis) nougat. It was this filling that rival Frank Mars used when creating his Milky Way. Meanwhile, Pendergast named their own nougat-filled bar the Fat Emma. They were originally planning to call it just Emma, but use of the Minnesota nougat inspired them to add an adjective that today would guarantee instant bankruptcy.

So while the Fat Emma used the same filling as the Milky Way, technically the Milky Way was not originally called the Fat Emma.

VERDICT: FALSE

At one stage the Fat Emma sold so well that Pendergast brought out a 'male version' called Pie Face.

The Bank of England was set up by a Scotsman

ALTHOUGH THE FIRST Governor of the Bank of England was Sir John Houblon – the descendant of a French Huguenot, who would appear on the £50 note issued 300 years later – the Bank was incorporated by Royal Charter in 1694 as a result of the efforts of one man in particular: William Paterson, who had by then established his name as a successful City businessman.

William Paterson was an enterprising Scot who devised a means to lend money to the government profitably – a government of fast-dwindling resources, due to King William III's war against France. Once Paterson's proposal had acquired the government's approval, with the backing of Chancellor of the Exchequer Charles Montagu, the plan was quickly put in place: 1,268 people collectively raised £1.2 million in under a fortnight in exchange for becoming shareholders in the all-new Bank of England. Oh, and they were also guaranteed an interest rate of 8 per cent.

The Bank gradually went on to assume more and more official powers, eventually issuing the country's notes, looking after its gold stash, managing the national debt, and assuming responsibility for financial and monetary stability; although the assignment of all these functions has changed over time.

Unfortunately for Paterson, it was pretty much all downhill after his big historic moment. By 1696 he had resigned from the

Bank after falling out with the other directors, and he returned north to help set up the Bank of Scotland, before coming up with the disastrous Darién Scheme to establish a Scottish colony in Panama.

VERDICT: TRUE
Before his Bank of England days it was rumoured, although never proven, that William Paterson had been a real-life pirate of the Caribbean.

No terrorist attack has ever been carried out on a Sunday

TERRORISM BY ITS NATURE tends to be directed at members of the public, so in terms of inflicting the maximum number of casualties, committing a terrorist act on a 'normal business day' is the most likely means to achieve this aim. In Western countries, the majority of the labour force work from Monday to Friday with relatively few working at the weekend, meaning that Sunday would not be the most effective day to target commuter trains, offices or busy shopping streets. However, in many countries, such as Israel and Islamic states, Sunday is of course a 'normal business day'. It therefore seems very unlikely that this claim would hold water.

So what about the hard facts? According to the MIPT Terrorism Knowledge Base, over 3,300 terrorist incidents have taken place on Sundays since records began in 1968. And historically Sunday isn't even the safest day: Saturday is the day of the week on which the fewest terrorist attacks have occurred, despite the fact that some of the highest-profile ones have happened on that day – for example, the Omagh bombing in Northern Ireland in 1998, and the Bali attacks in Indonesia in 2002.

So this is more an issue to do with perception and media reporting. A terrorist attack that is more 'successful' in terms of the number of fatalities will of course gain more media coverage than an incident in which no one dies – even when the terrorists' intention was the same. Likewise, the location and political significance of any attack will obviously affect its level of reporting.

VERDICT: FALSE

If you're the sort of person who will stay indoors based on the results of statistical analysis, make Wednesday your 'duvet day', as that is historically the most dangerous.

If the Nazis had managed to occupy Great Britain, Hitler was going to set up his London headquarters in Whiteley's shopping centre

William Whiteley set up his first business in London's Westbourne Grove in the 1860s, just around the corner from the Queensway shopping centre that now bears his name. After moving from Yorkshire to London he started out as a draper, before quickly building up his emporium and opening London's first department store. Famously he claimed to be the 'Universal Provider', able to supply anything from 'a pin to an elephant'. Desperate to live up to his promises, he successfully met one customer's demand for a pint of fleas.

The entrepreneur's various shops had a nasty habit of burning down, with the demise of the 1897 store being one of the biggest fires ever seen in the capital. The present building, in what was then known as Queen's Road, was built in 1911, although its form owes much to the redesign of 1925. It was acquired by Gordon Selfridge in 1927 and then by United Drapery Stores before becoming commercially unsustainable; after being shut down in 1981, the building was reopened eight years later in its current incarnation as a venue for shopping, eating and the movies.

By the time of the Second World War, William Whiteley himself was long gone, having been shot dead in the shop in 1907 by a man claiming to be his illegitimate son. Hitler is said to have specifically ordered the Luftwaffe not to bomb Whiteley's because he wanted it for his headquarters – on the basis that it was, quite simply, his favourite London building.

Unfortunately there does not seem to be any evidence to support this claim, and certainly nothing of the kind was uncovered by Linda Stratmann when researching her book *Whiteley's Folly*. The 'fact' becomes even more dubious when you consider that a similar claim has been made about the University of London's Senate House.

VERDICT: EXTREMELY SUSPECT

One of the plans mooted – very briefly – for the post-war redevelopment of the site was to build an international airport at the back of the building, right in the middle of Bayswater.

Claude Monet won the lottery

HISTORY'S ABIDING IMAGE of the doyen of Impressionism is that of an intense man (with a no less intense beard) whose paintings of landscapes, the Houses of Parliament and the water lilies at Giverny contributed to an artistic movement that changed the way we view the world. It is not the image of a man who pops down to his local corner shop to buy scratch cards, picks numbers based on his wife's birthday, and constantly checks Ceefax to see whether he's won the Thunderball draw.

Rather surprisingly, no lesser figure than the late Isaac Asimov would have you believe it. The sci-fi legend made the assertion in *Isaac Asimov's Book of Facts*, claiming that after Monet 'won 100,000 francs in the state lottery' he could afford to spend his time 'wandering about and painting the French countryside'.

Even more surprisingly, Asimov was not far off the mark – his only mistake was to pick the wrong artist. Armand Guillaumin, a less prominent Impressionist who was known to and mildly disliked by Monet, really did win 100,000 francs in the French state lottery in 1891, enabling him to finally quit the day job and focus on painting.

Perhaps Asimov was blinded by the amusing association of 'Monet' and 'money'; but we shouldn't be too hard on him. This was 1979, a time before the Internet, and a man who wrote over 400 books in a lifetime could be forgiven the occasional inaccuracy. Although that doesn't excuse him for making up facts like 'The phrase "What a guy!" is a cry of derision in Great Britain.'

VERDICT: FALSE

Monet did win, or rather lose, a very different kind of draw in 1860 when he was selected by lottery for military service in Algeria.

Florence Nightingale died of syphilis

THE POPULAR IMAGE OF THE 'lady with the lamp' is that of a saintly, clean-cut figure who followed a divine calling, selflessly devoting her life to the cause of nursing. However, many nurses today feel that this caricature trivialises the profession and represents an oversimplification of the life of a woman who had to fight against convention (at the time nursing was not regarded as a noble occupation for a woman of Florence Nightingale's wealthy background) and who made pioneering contributions not just to nursing care but to the use of statistics in epidemiology and public health.

On the other hand, the nursing profession probably doesn't want to be too closely associated with the idea of a bossy, opium-injecting layabout who hung out with prostitutes and drunks, kept an owl in her pocket and spent years lazing around in bed, while continually 'talking up' her illness so that she never had to do the washing-up. It has also frequently been suggested that Nightingale, who never married, was a lesbian, with particular regard to her cousin Marianne Nicholson. This isn't something that many people would regard as career-threateningly outrageous nowadays — okay, apart from the cousin bit, maybe — but Nightingale was living in the time of (and was closely associated with) Queen Victoria, who famously refused to accept that lesbianism could exist.

Nightingale certainly did suffer from poor health, something that has been the source of much speculation. In 1896 she was confined to bed, or more excessively a *chaise longue*, for the remaining fourteen years of her life — but she lived to the grand old age of 90. She published many incisive writings and worked extensively in her bedridden state, never exhibiting the mental debilitation associated with syphilis. There is absolutely no evidence to suggest she had the disease, with the originator of the claim believed to be a disgruntled priest who wanted to discredit Nightingale for 'not being religious enough'. The real causes of her condition — in all likelihood a combination of several different illnesses — possibly included brucellosis, fibromyalgia, post-traumatic stress disorder, chronic fatigue syndrome and a somewhat retrospective attribution of bipolar disorder.

VERDICT: FALSE

To further besmirch the reputation of Florence Nightingale, it should be noted that her name is an anagram of 'a long-feinting lecher'.

New Zealand is like England was 50 years ago

IS THIS BIZARRE CLAIM a compliment to New Zealand or an insult? There doesn't seem to be anything in the socio-economic data to support such a comparison (for example, the overall crime rate was proportionally similar for the two countries in 2005), so the assumption is that whoever tells you this is trying to make a general point about New Zealand's culture – or England's.

The 'fact' may be intended to suggest a nostalgic and fuzzy view of an age when life seemed to be simpler and more wholesome: you knew where you stood. Therefore, you'll be interested to learn that in New Zealand today, an average house costs just £2,000; bracken is still good for you (see p. 120); kids can play in the street without being subjected to 'lollipop rage'; Garth Brooks hasn't been born yet; you can drink-drive with impunity; and a soap opera called *The Archers* is a hit on the radio.

Before you jump on the first steamship over there, however, you should also be aware that there are some darker sides to today's New Zealand. They've only just stopped food rationing; they're still trying to figure out what teenagers are (see p. 200); everyone eats spam all the time; they actually think Bob Hope is funny; everything is in black-and-white; and a soap opera called *The Archers* is a hit on the radio. You have been warned.

VERDICT: BALDERDASH

With its yet-to-be-fully-developed tourist destinations and emerging democracy, Albania is, apparently, like Spain was 30 years ago.

The Romans made tea towels out of asbestos

ASBESTOS HAS TWO KEY PROPERTIES as far as humans are concerned. First, it is an excellent fire-retardant. Second, inhalation of its fibres can be lethal, causing asbestosis and a form of cancer called mesothelioma. So nowadays most types of asbestos are illegal in many countries – although in the case of the Canadian province of Quebec, the government is trying to ramp up the use of chrysotile asbestos.

In the ancient world – when cancer had only just been invented – the mineral was widely exploited for its fire-proof and high-tensile properties by the Greeks, Romans, Persians, Egyptians and, perhaps earliest of all, Scandinavians of the third millennium BC. However, that's not to say that there were no indications of the harmful side-effects of asbestos: it was known, for example, that slaves working in asbestos quarries were liable to die at a younger-than-average age.

From the surviving evidence it seems that the Romans found the most diverse applications of asbestos, incorporating it into building materials, clothing, candle-wicks, burial shrouds, tablecloths, tea towels (dish towels), napkins and other linen. When he'd finally finished naming civilisations after dogs (see p. 247), Pliny described how he had seen asbestos napkins cleaned more thoroughly than could be achieved with water, by throwing them on a fire to burn off any stains. On the other hand, Pliny also claimed that asbestos grew in the deserts of India surrounded by serpents. With this calibre of pub fact, Pliny would have made an excellent drinking companion.

VERDICT: TRUE

You may also be told how Charlemagne – the first Holy Roman Emperor – would amaze his dinner guests by chucking an asbestos tablecloth into the fire, pulling it back out again, whiter than white, and then claiming it was 'magic', like some kind of David Blaine washing-powder endorsement; sadly, however, there is no evidence to suggest this ever actually happened.

SPORTS

George Foreman named all his children 'George'

THIS CLAIM IS especially noteworthy when you realise that the former heavyweight boxing champion has ten children – of which half are female.

The boys really are all named George. To avoid the inevitable confusion they are called, in descending order of age, George Jr, George III, George IV, George V and, you guessed it, George VI. Sadly, when it came to the girls, Big George let us down. Two of them are *nearly* named George – Freeda George and Georgetta – but the remaining three are Michi, Natalie and Leola.

The boxer-turned-minister, who calls his fifth wife Joan even though her real name is Mary, has given differing reasons for his naming strategy. He told *Ebony* magazine in 1995 that it was because he himself only discovered his real father when he was in his late twenties – so he wanted his boys 'to have something to know one another' and have 'a name that they could run into whenever they had problems or if they ever got lost'. Interviewed for CBS's *The Early Show* in 2005, he joked that because he'd been hit in the head so many times in his boxing career, it was a tactic to avoid having to remember lots of different names.

Never lacking in humour, his children's book *Let George Do It!* (written with Fran Manushkin) tells the story of a father named Big George who gets into all sorts of confusion because he has five sons named George.

VERDICT: HALF TRUE

In the same *Early Show* interview, George Sr claimed that his famous Lean Mean Grilling Machine was 'the most successful electrical appliance ever in the history of London, England'.

The guy who went over Niagara Falls in a barrel died after slipping on an orange peel

IN THE TWO-DIMENSIONAL, childlike world of cartoons, magnets are always horseshoe-shaped. There is a pleasing synergy here, since the Horseshoe Falls at Niagara have long been a magnet for two-dimensional timewasters who equate childlike attention-seeking with admirable bravery. Everyone else just thinks they're stupid, only watching in the hope that a video of the 'stunt' will net £500 from *You've Been Framed*.

As for 'the guy' who went over, there have actually been many barrel-based attempts. Given that such ventures are usually powered by nothing more than the river current and testosterone, it is surprising that the first, in 1901, was by a woman aged 63. Annie Taylor was stuffed into a mattress-padded pickle barrel; battered but buoyant, she survived.

The second attempt was by the Cornishman Bobby Leach in 1911, using a steel barrel. He survived, although he broke both kneecaps and his jaw. Fourteen years later, during a tour of Australia and New Zealand, he slipped on an orange peel as he walked down the street in Christchurch. A resulting gangrene infection killed him.

The very first 'stunt' at the falls was a barbaric incident in which a dilapidated schooner was loaded with 'animals of the most ferocious kind, such as Panthers, Wild Cats and Wolves' – in reality a buffalo, two bears, two raccoons, a dog and a goose – and set adrift above the falls, watched by a crowd of ten thousand warped spectators in 1827. The goose was the only animal to survive the plunge, while the two bears ingeniously escaped before the schooner went over the edge and swam to Goat Island.

VERDICT: TRUE
The good news is that if 'daredevils' survive, the idiots can be fined up to $10,000.

More people die angling than in any other sport

ANGLING IS A SPORT DESIGNED to give men an excuse to spend Sundays away from their wives and other female family members. The day can be spent in quiet, uncommunicative contemplation of life, sometimes accompanied by a can or two of Special Brew and some ham sandwiches (prepared earlier by the wife). On a good day, if the light holds, you can spend up to ten hours without having to speak to anyone, although you may sometimes have to give a silent nod of understanding to other men engaged in the same pursuit.

Another aspect of angling involves the use of a rod and line to catch fish. This can be for the purposes of eating, or simply the primordial pleasure of mastering the spectacular and mysterious forces of nature in a poorly dredged canal alongside an industrial estate.

It is the fact that angling is a solitary activity undertaken outdoors that makes it so dangerous. In more overtly physical sports such as boxing, rugby or Australian Rules there will be paramedics on hand in case things get really bad; although in the case of American Football, they're never needed since it's played by a bunch of scaredy-cats with power-dressing shoulder pads and protective helmets who have to stop for a rest every ten seconds.

With angling, however, you're susceptible to storms, flash

floods and lightning, getting your line caught in overhead power cables, and – more significantly – the possibility of drowning with no one around to help.

Notice that this claim is not expressed as a proportion of the number of people taking part in a sport – in other words, it's the fact that angling is so popular that accounts for its high death toll (24 in the UK in 2002, according to the Royal Society for the Prevention of Accidents); yet this was exceeded by fatalities in the sport of swimming. Figures from Water Safety New Zealand show that in 2004 even kayaking was more lethal than angling.

VERDICT: FALSE

Deadpan comic Steven Wright – who, like Woody Allen, seems to have a quote about everything – is attributed with the claim, 'There's a fine line between fishing and standing on the shore like an idiot.'

VfL Wolfsburg used to be managed by Wolfgang Wolf

VFL WOLFSBURG IS a German football team that, as the name suggests, is based in the city of Wolfsburg in Lower Saxony. (The VfL bit stands for *Verein für Leibesübungen*: 'club for physical exercise'.) There is a pleasingly wolf-based quality to the name of Wolfgang Wolf, who managed the club – nicknamed the Wolves – from 1998 to 2003.

The player-turned-manager would have been sufficiently well known that letters addressed simply to 'Wolfgang Wolf, Wolfsburg' would have been delivered. Not leaving such matters to chance, English comedian James Rogers renamed himself Boothby Graffoe, after the Lincolnshire village where he once lived, and also renamed his house Boothby Graffoe – so that letters would be addressed to 'Boothby Graffoe, Boothby Graffoe, Boothby Graffoe'.

The Wolves, meanwhile, play in the Volkswagen Arena, with

the club itself 90 per cent owned by the car manufacturer. If this seems like a curious investment, it's because the city owes its whole existence to Volkswagen, having started life in 1938 as KdF-Stadt. KdF, or *Kraft durch Freude* ('strength through joy'), was the name of the leisure section of the Third Reich's national labour organisation; among other activities, they promoted the concept of the affordable *Volkswagen* ('people's car'). Adolf Hitler dictated that the car, later to become nicknamed the Beetle, should be manufactured in a purpose-built community. After the war, KdF-Stadt was rebranded as Wolfsburg, the name of a local castle.

Wolfsburg's relative youth and industrial background have created something of an image problem and, until the recent opening of the phæno science museum, it has struggled to attract tourists, except for hardcore car fetishists. English tourists contemplating where to take next year's holidays may wish to consider that Wolfsburg is twinned with Luton.

VERDICT: TRUE
Shunning wolves in favour of bears, Wolfsburg's ice hockey team is Grizzly Adams EHC Wolfsburg.

'Golf' originally stood for 'gentlemen only, ladies forbidden'

THE MAN IN THE PUB, who's probably never been near a golf course in his life, will assure you that the first club house in Scotland had a sign over the door declaring 'gentlemen only, ladies forbidden'; and that the acronym 'GOLF' gradually became the name of the sport. This is absolutely bogus.

The earliest written reference to the game is in a 1457 decree by Scotland's King James II banning golf and football. Sadly, this utopian dream didn't last, and within a few years everyone was at it – apart from the women, of course. The fifteenth century was not exactly a time when the English language was notable for its acronyms, and the fact that the earliest recorded forms of the word were written as 'gouff', 'goiff' and 'goff', not just 'golf', rule out an acronym as the origin. There is of course not a shred of evidence for the 'gentlemen only, ladies forbidden' claim, but no one knows the real derivation of the word. Two possible etymologies include the medieval Dutch *'kolf'* ('club', though evidence is sketchy) and the fact that some modern Scots dialects use the word *'gowf'* ('blow' or 'strike').

In any case, why on earth would the club house owners need to specify both 'gentlemen only' *and* 'ladies forbidden', which mean the same thing? Perhaps they thought: 'This as-yet-unnamed game we're playing is bound to be named after this sign. If we just call it "ladies forbidden" it'll be unpronounceable, but if we call it "gentlemen only" it'd get confused with the Asian board game Go.' Maybe not.

VERDICT: FALSE

In 2006 Professor Ling Hongling of Lanzhou University controversially claimed that golf, or *'chuiwan'*, was first played in China in AD 945.

Adidas and PUMA were founded by two brothers who didn't talk to each other for nearly 30 years

IN AN AGE OF GLOBAL brand awareness and transnational corporations, it may seem surprising that rival sportswear manufacturers Adidas and PUMA would both have their headquarters in the same Bavarian town of Herzogenaurach. But it's true: brothers Adolf and Rudolf Dassler set up a shoe-making business there in 1924 under the name Gebrüder Dassler Schuhfabrik (the Dassler Brothers Shoe Factory).

Business boomed and by 1936 they had persuaded Jesse Owens to compete in Dassler shoes at the Berlin Olympics. But by the Second World War, when they were selling 200,000 pairs of shoes a year, tensions between the two brothers were becoming more and more acute. The exact reasons are not clear, but in 1948 things came to a crunch and following a violent feud the brothers decided to split, with two companies emerging. Adolf set up Adidas (taken from 'Adi', the abbreviated version of his first name, and 'Das' from Dassler) while Rudolf established PUMA (probably in reference to the athletic capabilities of the big cat).

For the next 26 years the two brothers were bitter enemies who never exchanged a word, constantly trying to out-do each other when it came to celebrity endorsements and market share. With the two firms based in the same town, things became tricky, to the extent that there were 'Adidas bars' and 'PUMA bars' with mutually exclusive clienteles. Nowadays rivalry is a little less bitter.

Rudi Dassler died in 1974, with Adi outliving him by four

years; they seemingly took the exact reason for their feud to their graves.

VERDICT: TRUE
During the 1990s Adidas was run by Robert Louis-Dreyfus, cousin of Julia Louis-Dreyfus who played Elaine in the classic sitcom *Seinfeld*.

Pope John Paul II used to be a goalkeeper

AS A YOUNG MAN, Karol Józef Wojtyła enjoyed a good kick-about in his home town of Wadowice. There were normally two football teams split loosely along religious lines – with the future Pope often playing in goal for the Jewish side against the Catholics, due to a shortage of players. It has been suggested that his closeness to the Jewish community in 1930s Poland formed the background for his subsequent attempts to forge closer relations between the Catholic and Jewish faiths.

It is intriguing to picture the head of the Catholic Church pacing angrily up and down the goal line, shouting vapid foot-ballisms like 'Create the space!', 'Work for the ball!' and 'Man on!', while occasionally clapping his thickly gloved hands together. This is rather at odds with our image of the frail Pope later in life, when his fans would be more likely to chant 'Ave Maria' than 'Who Ate All the Pies?'

John Paul II was in mixed company when it came to other goalkeepers who went on to find fame in non-sports arenas. David Icke played in goal for Coventry City and Hereford United before

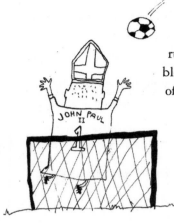

later describing himself as the son of God and claiming that the world is run by a shadowy elite of shape-shifting, blood-drinking reptiles. And the beliefs of the existentialist writer Albert Camus, goalie for the University of Algiers team, would be of concern to any Pope. But maybe JP2 could take heart in the songs of Julio Iglesias (formerly goalkeeper for Real Madrid), as his surname means 'churches' in Spanish.

VERDICT: BACK OF THE NET!

John Paul II remained an enthusiastic sports fan throughout his life: he continued to ski and swim while in office, and he once blessed the Ferrari Formula One team.

It costs $25,000 for a permit to climb Mount Everest

AS YOU PROBABLY KNOW, Mount Everest, straddling the border between Nepal and Tibet, is the highest mountain on earth. What you may not have known is that the place is treated like the ultimate theme park ride, with a massive commercial operation fleecing climbers and hapless tourists to the tune of $25,000 a go (at that rate, you can only begin to imagine how much they charge for a hotdog when you get to the top). Oh yeah, and despite the fact that the permit is issued by Nepal, the 'sky-high' charge is a perfectly round US dollar amount.

Actually, it's true. Apart from the bit about there being hotdogs at the top.

If you're foolhardy enough to climb Mount Everest – nearly 10 per cent of those attempting the summit never make it back alive – it'll cost you something chronic. First of all there's the cost of getting there, with the usual practice (once you've got to Nepal) being to fly from Kathmandu to Lukla and then trek for a week or so to Base Camp. Then you'll have to shell out thousands of dollars for food, fuel, sherpas, cooks, yaks, equipment, medical supplies and (unless you're seriously experienced or seriously deluded) oxygen. Don't forget: some warm clothing may come in handy too.

It costs $100 to enter the Sagarmatha National Park (Sagarmatha is the Nepalese name for Everest, hurriedly invented in the 1960s when they suddenly realised they didn't have a name for it), plus another couple of thousand to cross the Khumbu Icefall. There's also a $4,000 'garbage management' deposit, which you get back when you return, assuming that you haven't strewn empty cans of Tennent's Super all the way up the side of the mountain, and assuming that you do actually return. By far the biggest administrative cost, however, is the climbing permit issued by the Ministry of Culture, Tourism and Civil Aviation. A solo permit costs $25,000 (though they do generously allow you to pay the equivalent value in rupees), with various 'bulk buy' discounts up to a team of seven costing $70,000. That's if you ascend via the south-east ridge; any other route and it's a flat $50,000 – take it or leave it.

You can also climb Everest from Tibet (where they call it

Qomolangma), via the north-east ridge. To do this, the Chinese permit costs a bargain-basement $5,000 for an expedition of up to ten climbers – but the ascent from Tibet is so treacherous that it makes the south-east ridge look about as challenging as a Monopoly pub crawl.

VERDICT: TRUE
When the height of the mountain was first measured in the 1850s and found to be exactly 29,000 feet, 'they' announced its official height as 29,002 feet so that it didn't sound made-up.

Basketball was invented by the Aztecs

NO, COLLEGE SPORTS FANATICS, this doesn't mean that basketball was invented at San Diego State University; the suggestion is that the sport of basketball – or something like it – originated in the pre-Columbian civilisations of Mesoamerica.

Conquistadors and other European visitors to Central America were bemused in the sixteenth century to witness games of tlachtli, or ullamaliztli (meaning 'ballgame' in Nahuatl), which survives in a few areas of Mexico to this day as the game of hip ulama. But even by the time the Spanish turned up, ullamaliztli was already about three thousand years old, having been played by the Mayans and Olmecs as well as the Aztecs.

A lot is known about the Aztecs' version of 'basketball', from the modern-day conventions of hip ulama and extensive archaeo-logical evidence, including courts, balls and figurines of players. The game was played on an I-shaped court with a long oblong

centre court and a smaller court at each
end. Players had to get a rubber ball
into a raised stone hoop – but using
only their hips and knees (or, in
some versions of the game, other
body parts and sticks). If you lost,
you stood a pretty good chance of
being decapitated and sacrificed
to the gods.

Credit for the game of basketball as
it is known today goes to James
Naismith, a PE teacher at what is now
Springfield College in Massachusetts,
who was tasked with giving his students something to do indoors
during the winter months. He seems to have overlooked the mul-
titude of existing options, such as smoking, drinking, poker and
darts, and instead used the materials available to him and created
a game in which a football ('soccer ball') had to be dunked into
peach baskets.

VERDICT: TRUE
What are peach baskets, anyway?

None of The Beach Boys could surf

IN 1961 BROTHERS Brian, Carl and Dennis Wilson, their
cousin Mike Love and their friend Al Jardine formed a band.
Looking for inspiration for original material to record, Dennis –

at that time the hanger-on of the band, who had to learn the drums in order to find something to do — suggested that Brian should write a song about surfing. Brian agreed, and he must have agonised for hours before deciding on the title of 'Surfin'', which became their first single. By the time it was released, the band had become The Beach Boys, cashing in on the sun, surf 'n' girls image of Californian culture. It was also much better than their earlier name, The Pendletones, a pun inspired by a brand of shirt.

The fact that the suggestion came from Dennis is no coincidence, since he was the only member of the group who was obsessed with the beach and surfing in general. Once commenting that he didn't understand why everyone didn't live at the beach (they tried that in Benidorm and look what happened), Dennis was a regular surfer. He was the only one in the group who could 'properly' surf, while the rest were a bunch of kooks — although it's possible that Brian once tried to pull a roundhouse cutback on a boogie board, before doing a wettie warmer in the Pope's living room.

In 1983 Dennis Wilson's beach-bum lifestyle came to an abrupt end when he drowned while drunkenly swimming in Marina del Ray, Los Angeles. He was diving at the spot where his yacht, *Harmony*, used to be berthed before it was repossessed, trying to find items he had previously thrown overboard. This should be a stark reminder to anyone about the dangers of drink-diving.

VERDICT: FALSE

After New York, Benidorm is the city with the most skyscrapers in the world.

After being deposed, Idi Amin became a sports reporter

DURING THE EIGHT YEARS of his brutal dictatorship, Idi Amin oversaw a regime responsible for the murder of hundreds of thousands of people; he expelled all Asians from Uganda in 1972; and he apparently had a Chief Justice killed for releasing a European who had been charged with 'stealing a telephone directory from a hotel'. So hardly the kind of guy you'd expect to find cheerily shouting 'booya!' from a commentary box.

On the other hand, he was something of a sportsman: he was an accomplished swimmer and footballer, and for most of the 1950s he was the Ugandan light heavyweight boxing champion. (For those of us who know nothing about boxing, apparently 'light heavyweight' is a perfectly sensible phrase.) Equally, he was completely unpredictable in his behaviour, very probably the result of mental illness, declaring himself King of Scotland and describing himself as 'Lord of All the Beasts of the Earth and Fish of the Sea, and Conqueror of the British Empire in Africa in General and Uganda in Particular'. So perhaps he just wanted to try something new in general, and one of those microphones that you can lean against your upper lip in particular.

In reality, the kilt-wearing despot didn't go near the sports commentary business after exile in 1979. His first destination was Libya, but after falling out with Colonel Gadaffi – perhaps because Amin's full title was longer than Libya's (see p. 250) – he decided to move to Saudi Arabia, where he spent the rest of his life in quiet, state-sponsored luxury.

VERDICT: FALSE

In 1973 Idi Amin set up a Save Britain Fund to help resolve the UK's economic crisis; after it was rejected, he then offered to mediate in the Northern Ireland peace talks.

Teenagers get less exercise than pensioners

IT'S GENERALLY ACCEPTED that in Western societies at least, kids have become progressively lazier and fatter over the last 50 years or so. It's not like in their grandparents' time, when you'd think nothing of walking 80 miles for a pint of milk, and when gym class consisted of schoolboys engaging in naked bare-knuckle boxing in freezing-cold conditions.

Let's not be too harsh on teenagers though: in their grandparents' time, they didn't even exist (see p. 200). Nowadays, not only do they exist, but they often moodily wish they didn't; and moreover, they've discovered all sorts of concepts like 'Why walk when you can take the car?' and 'Why read a book when you can watch the film?'

The International Obesity Taskforce – yes, there is such a thing – estimated in a report submitted to the World Health Organization in 2004 that in Brazil and the USA, an additional 0.5 per cent of the child population was becoming overweight each year, with the rate being nearer to 1 per cent each year in Canada, Australia and parts of Europe.

The reasons why teenagers nowadays are lardier than previous generations is not entirely clear. It's not as if TV or cheeseburgers are recent inventions, although perhaps gaming consoles and the

Internet are newer reasons to stay indoors. Interestingly, however, a 2002 study by the UK's Institute for Social and Economic Research found that people with Internet access at home were *more* likely to play sports than those without. Maybe the discovery of just how tedious the Internet is prompts them to leave the house – while the rest mope about at home wondering what on earth 'blogging' and 'podcasts' are.

Gran!

To back up everyone's 'gut' feelings: the same study found that people of pensionable age spent a third more time each day doing physical activity than youngsters (1 hour and 40 minutes compared to 1 hour and 15 minutes). Furthermore, almost a quarter of the lazy, bone-idle, good-for-nothing teenagers did 'no physical activity lasting more than five minutes on an average day'.

VERDICT: TRUE

The study in question was commissioned by BBC News (an organisation that you might think should be reporting news, not generating it) and drew on data from the National Survey of Time Use – it's not difficult to think of better ways to use time than on conducting national surveys.

There's a rifle range in the House of Lords

THE PALACE OF WESTMINSTER, also known as the Houses of Parliament, is a vast complex comprising nearly 1,200 rooms. Encompassing the House of Commons, the House of Lords, Westminster Hall and Big Ben, the various buildings represent a self-contained village boasting all the facilities MPs and Lords could need, so that they never have to venture into the real world outside: two post offices, restaurants and private dining rooms, over ten different bars, two main libraries, a travel agent, a car park and seven times as many cash machines as are said to be in Albania (see p. 277).

According to the 2006 House of Lords staff handbook, all persons (not just politicians) permanently employed at the Palace of Westminster are entitled to join the Houses of Parliament Sports and Social Club, giving them access to 'a bar with hot and cold snacks, darts, and a 0.22 rifle range'. At lunchtime the place is probably packed out with elderly parliamentarians smeared in warpaint and snacking on hot nuts while loosing off volleys of gunfire into silhouettes of prominent journalists.

Before you think you might get tooled up and take the opportunity to pump a few rounds into the wall of a world-famous London landmark, bear in mind that details of the rifle range and its users are extremely shadowy. Enquiries from the public are met with dignified silence (not entirely surprising, from a security point of view), and even within the Palace there are no directions to the out-of-the-way location, directly underneath the House of Lords chamber, with access via a secure door. The current captain of the Commons Rifle Club is rumoured to be the bow-tie-toting

Labour MP Martyn Jones; as for peers, following the death of former international marksman Lord Swansea in 2005 it was said that the Lords shooting team had been disbanded entirely.

VERDICT: TRUE
The modernising and inclusive attitude of British politicians was highlighted in 1994 when they voted to keep the rifle range rather than open a crèche.

The bloke who invented jogging died while jogging

THIS IS A WELL-KNOWN 'FACT' quoted by all couch potatoes, heavy smokers and binge drinkers to justify the amount of time spent down the pub and/or their hatred of physical activity of any kind. It seems too good to be true, doesn't it?

First of all, can anyone really be credited with having 'invented' jogging? Technically, perhaps not – but it's beyond doubt that in the 1970s there was one man who advocated jogging as the new quick-fix for all ills. Astonishingly, his name was Jim Fixx (no relation to Sir Jimmy Savile). He wrote the best-seller *The Complete Book of Running*, which prompted suburban dads everywhere to dig out their dodgy shorts and Dunlop green stripe plimsolls, and run round the block of an evening to 'work off' those four lunchtime pints. (In the 1970s, everyone went to the pub at lunchtime – FACT.)

Yes, Mr Fixx died of a massive heart attack in July 1984 while jogging in Vermont; he was only 52. The autopsy revealed that one of his coronary arteries was clogged to the horrifying level of 95 per cent.

VERDICT: SATISFYINGLY TRUE

This clearly proves it doesn't matter how much you jog if you feast on pie and chips every day.

All the cricket balls in the world originate from a single factory in Kent

THE QUINTESSENTIALLY ENGLISH GAME of cricket is said to have begun in the county of Kent, so if there was a single factory churning out cricket balls, that's where you'd logically expect it to be based. A number of cricket-ball makers previously based in Kent have since relocated, merged or closed down; but they have not all been superseded by one huge factory, furiously working 24 hours a day to meet the world's cricketing needs, popping balls from tubes like something out of a Dr Seuss story.

Predictably, the location of cricket-ball makers mirrors the regions in which cricket is extensively played, and these areas in turn correspond to the countries of the world once under the influence of the British Empire. For example, there are numerous cricket-ball manufacturers in India, one of which is the intriguingly named Sanspareils Greenlands, makers of the only ball approved for official use in Indian international test and one-day matches. (If you don't know anything about cricket, think of a 'test' as a soul-destroyingly slow game stretched out over several boring days, and a 'one-day international' as equally boring but shorter, with the players forced to wear undignified coloured pyjamas in exchange for money.)

The biggest manufacturer of cricket balls in the world is Kookaburra Sport, which, as its name suggests, is an Australian company. Their Turf Cricket Ball has been used for test cricket matches involving Australia, New Zealand and South Africa since 1946.

Back in Kent the ball-making tradition is kept alive in the form of Alfred Reader & Co, based in Teston, where cricket balls have been produced since the mid-nineteenth century, and Dukes, who go back even further.

VERDICT: FALSE

Apparently a cricketer's repulsive practice of rubbing a cricket ball up and down his crotch is to give the ball 'swing'; even more revoltingly, cricket rules say that you can only use saliva or sweat to assist the polishing process.

Arthur Conan Doyle introduced skiing to Switzerland

WHILE SCOTLAND – birthplace of the creator of Sherlock Holmes – has some pretty mountainous areas, it's no match for the Swiss Alps when it comes to height or snow coverage. The fact that Arthur Conan Doyle spent most of his life in the south of England makes this claim even more bizarre.

In 1893 Conan Doyle's wife Louise ('Touie') was diagnosed with TB and given just months to live. Believing that the Swiss mountain air would do her good, the couple moved to Davos – which paid off, as Touie lived for another thirteen years, though they returned to England in 1896.

A massive sports fan, Conan Doyle was racking his brains as to what sorts of outdoor shenanigans he could get up to, when he heard about the Branger brothers: two saddlers who had recently received 'the first Norwegian snow shoes in Switzerland'. After some intensive training, Conan Doyle helped the Branger brothers' publicity effort when the three of them completed a seven-hour ski trek to Arosa, over an avalanche-prone pass, to the amazement of sceptical locals.

Conan Doyle wrote an account of the journey for readers of *The Strand* magazine back home. (This proved to be an ideal opportunity to debunk a pub fact recounted to him by his tailor, that 'Harris tweed cannot wear out.')

The Branger brothers had clearly started skiing in Switzerland shortly before Conan Doyle's arrival, but his achievement – commemorated by a plaque near the ice stadium at Davos – was to introduce and popularise the idea of skiing as a leisure activity, which would enhance Switzerland's status as a tourist destination, particularly for the British.

VERDICT: TRUE

Perhaps another role model for Pope John Paul II (see p. 227), Arthur Conan Doyle was the first goalkeeper for Portsmouth FC.

You have to be dead to appear on a British postage stamp (apart from Roger Taylor out of Queen)

ANYONE WHO'S LOOKED at British stamps will notice that the reigning monarch quite clearly appears on every single one, even if only in a slightly dated silhouette profile. Since by definition the reigning monarch can't be dead, this fact cannot be true. However, it has long been a rule of the Royal Mail that the only living people who may be visibly identifiable on stamps are members of the royal family – which explains why Charles and Diana were allowed on a stamp to celebrate their wedding in 1981.

Nevertheless, in 2005 this rule was shamelessly abandoned in the name of cricket, to commemorate the England team's Ashes victory over Australia. (For those fortunate enough to live in non-cricketing nations, 'the Ashes' is a two-team competition between England and Australia that seems to happen at bafflingly irregular intervals, and which is about as exciting as wondering whether someone's baby will turn out to be a boy or a girl.) The four stamps consist primarily of teeth-baring smiles beaming from the clearly identifiable faces of Michael Vaughan, Kevin Pietersen and the 'hilariously' nicknamed Andrew 'Freddie' Flintoff (hey, have you ever noticed that 'Flintoff' sounds a bit like 'Flintstone'?!).

So what's with the Roger Taylor disclaimer? In 1999 the Royal Mail issued a series of 'millennium stamps', of which one depicted the late Freddie Mercury. The Queen frontman was already deemed a controversial choice by some members of the British public (even though he was a hardcore philatelist whose stamp collection was posthumously auctioned off to the Royal Mail), but fury ensued when it became clear that a tiny Roger Taylor was just about visible behind the drums in the background.

VERDICT: FALSE

The United Kingdom is the only country in the world that doesn't print the name of the issuing country on its stamps – even Libya manages to cram its name on (see p. 250).

GEOGRAPHY

There are no piers in Scotland

THIS SEEMS EXTREMELY UNLIKELY, given the number of islands in Scotland that aren't big enough to justify substantially sized ports and harbours, and sure enough, it's completely untrue. To pick just one example: the Isle of Colonsay, in the Inner Hebrides, is served by a ferry that berths at Scalasaig pier on the eastern side of the island.

What about piers on the mainland? Again, plenty, of course. The Caithness town of Wick, in the north-east of Scotland, has a North River Pier and a South River Pier. Inland, too, Scotland's waters boast many: Loch Lomond, for example, has around fifteen private and public piers and jetties around its shores.

So how could this 'fact' have originated? Most likely it started out as a claim specific to *pleasure piers* – structures built out into the sea for the amusement of holidaymakers looking to enjoy a stroll in the sea air, stuff their faces with chips and mushy peas, and occasionally jump off the end in ill-conceived birdman competitions.

There used to be a pleasure pier at Portobello (once a separate resort town, but now a suburb of Edinburgh). The pier was built by the luckless Thomas Bouch, designer of the original Tay Bridge, which fell into the river along with a passenger train in 1879. But Portobello pier was demolished in 1917 – so today, unlike England and Wales, which have many surviving recreational piers from the Victorian heyday of the seaside holiday, Scotland does not have any pleasure piers.

VERDICT: FALSE

The pleasure pier at Southend-on-Sea in Essex remains the longest pleasure pier in the world, despite a serious fire in October 2005.

There's a park bench in Bristol that has its own postcode

THE REASON FOR GIVING SOMEWHERE a postcode is to designate a particular destination for the delivery of mail. So who needs to send anything to a park bench in the west of England? And wouldn't any letters sent there just blow away in the first gust of wind, to be swept up in a vortex of dead leaves and crisp packets, coming to rest next to a dirty carrier bag high up in a tree?

The answer lies in the use of postcodes to identify addresses for administrative purposes like credit-checking and general form-filling. In the case of the UK's venerable but bureaucratically corpulent National Health Service, it is not possible for individuals to register with a doctor unless they can provide details of their home address, complete with postcode. When it comes to offering medical assistance to rough sleepers this becomes a problem, with the traditional solution being to re-register the same patient as 'temporarily visiting the area'.

The Montpelier Health Centre in Bristol decided to 'address' the situation by using 'Park Bench, Portland Square' as a residence to permanently register homeless patients, so that they could benefit from better continuity of care. However, following negative publicity about

the situation in 2000, the local health authority thought long and hard and agreed that 'No fixed address, c/o Montpelier Health Centre' could be used instead.

Hats off to the NHS genius who finally cracked it! Let's see it again: 'No fixed address, c/o Montpelier Health Centre'. There are surely few people alive in the world today with the intellectual capacity to achieve such a conceptual breakthrough, when the alternative option – to postcode a park bench – seems so obvious.

VERDICT: PAST ITS FACT-BY DATE

Just for the record, the postcode in question was BS2 8QD, but nowadays this is used for a block of flats on nearby Wilder Street.

The name 'Graham' comes from the town of Grantham

GRAHAMS EVERYWHERE MIGHT PANIC if this is the first time they've realised what sort of place they may be named after (see p. 261). Initially they can take comfort in the fact that the use of Graham or Graeme as a first name derives from a Scottish surname. But could the Scots actually be named after Margaret Thatcher's home town?

Clan Graham folklore tells of a Caledonian chieftain called Grame, Greme, Graym, or Gryme, of either Danish or Pictish descent, who is said to have successfully attacked the Roman army, driving them back from the Antonine Wall down to Hadrian's Wall. If true, this family line then disappeared, perhaps through marriage into Scottish or Danish royalty, or it may have been later absorbed into the Anglo-Norman Grahams, starting with William de Graham, who is regarded as the first 'proven' Graham in Scotland. A member of the household of Scotland's King David I, he moved to Scotland after David ascended to the throne in 1124, and settled in lands granted to him around Abercorn and Dalkeith.

William's family are believed to have come to England with William the Conqueror, and owned the manor of the town known nowadays as Grantham, or the heroin capital of Lincolnshire. In medieval times Grantham was written variously as Graham, Grandham and Granham (and is itself thought to mean either 'Granta's village' or 'gravel village' in Old English). When William left Grantham – which was probably as soon as he possibly could – he was known as de Graham, to indicate his origins.

VERDICT: TRUE

The Clan Graham motto is '*ne oublie*', 'never forget': perhaps in this case they could make an exception.

The Canary Islands are named after a dog

THE CANARY ISLANDS ARE DEFINITELY *not* named after a bird. In fact, it was the other way round: the canary is a member of the finch family indigenous to the Canary Islands, and was named to reflect its origins. So what's with the dog?

The English-language name for the islands derives from the Spanish *Las Islas Canarias*. The Spanish took control of the islands in the fifteenth century after much local resistance, but they were not the first to name them. For that we must turn to the Roman scholar Pliny the Elder. In Book VI of his only surviving work, the *Historia Naturalis*, he reports on the findings of an expedition sent to investigate the 'Fortunate Isles' by King Juba II of Numidia and Mauretania (Cleopatra and Mark Antony's son-in-law, no less). According to Pliny, one of the islands was home to a breed of large dog; he explains that the island was therefore known as *Canaria* (after the Latin word for dog, *canis*).

While *Canaria* originally referred to a single island, by the fourth century AD the Romans were using the name *Canariæ insulæ* to describe what we know today as the Canary Islands. There are two dogs on the islands' modern-day coat of arms in reference to the origin of the name.

Mystery solved. Except that, unbelievably, there was a tribe of North African Berbers known as the Canarii or Canarios – also mentioned by Pliny (in Book V), who said this was because they shared the same food as dogs. These people are believed by some to have settled on Gran Canaria during the third millennium BC. Coincidence?

VERDICT: TRUE
The canary bird was originally greenish-brown and was bred in Europe to make it more yellow.

Khartoum, the capital city of Sudan, means 'elephant's trunk'

THIS FACT WOULD probably be more widely known – and hence less entertaining – if Sudan was the sort of place likely to attract lots of holidaymakers, as it would be the first thing you'd read in the Khartoum section of the travel guide. However, there are virtually no guides (the 2005 Bradt guide being a lone exception), though there is a *Rough Guide to the Music of Sudan* album and there are numerous travel websites telling you about the place – probably very useful when you're strolling around Darfur with your MP3 player, trying to get an Internet connection on your WiFi-enabled PDA. Basically, decades of civil war and a 1998 cruise-missile attack by the US have put visitors off.

All of which is a shame (rather more so for the people involved in the fighting than for overfed tourists looking to top up their tans) since Sudan, the largest country in Africa, is rich in cultural and archaeological heritage, corresponding to the ancient kingdom of Nubia.

Back to the elephant's trunk, or '*ra's al-hurtum*' in Arabic, a corruption of which became Khartoum. The main city, established as an Egyptian military outpost in 1821, lies to the south of the confluence of the Blue Nile and the White Nile, and is linked by bridges to Khartoum North and Omdurman on the other banks, collectively forming Sudan's largest conurbation. If you look at a map or satellite image of the city, apparently the confluence of the Nile tributaries *sort of could look a bit like* an elephant's trunk, *if* you'd had a few too many beers. That's the derivation, but it's not at all convincing.

VERDICT: TRUE

There are more pyramids in Sudan than there are in its northern neighbour Egypt.

There's a town in New Mexico called Truth or Consequences

As RIDICULOUS AS IT SEEMS – in fact, as ridiculous as it *is* – there really is a place called Truth or Consequences, New Mexico. It may strike you, particularly if you're not well versed in American broadcasting history, as a completely surreal name for a town: perhaps in the old days some pioneer had a moment of epiphany and realised that there was no going back. On the other hand, when you discover that it's named after a radio quiz show, it may just strike you as a bit tawdry.

The Sierra County town, on the banks of the Rio Grande, was originally called Hot Springs. All that changed in 1950 when

Ralph Edwards, presenter of the popular radio programme *Truth or Consequences* (and also famous for fronting *This Is Your Life*), decided to 'honour' a location in America by renaming it to celebrate the show's tenth anniversary. The Hot Springs Chamber of Commerce thought it would be a great way for the town to boost tourism and shed its relative anonymity: there are at least five other towns in the US called Hot Springs. The majority of residents were in favour of the change and the name has been retained to this day.

In 2006 Truth or Consequences ('T or C' to locals) had a population of around 7,200, with a growing proportion of older people. The New Mexico Tourism Department says that it is a popular location for retirees, with the town recently being named by *Where To Retire* magazine – 'America's foremost authority on retirement relocation' – as one of the country's top retirement destinations.

VERDICT: TRUTH AND CONSEQUENCES

At least they didn't rename themselves after the long-running quiz show made famous by Art Linkletter, *People Are Funny*.

The official name of Libya is the longest country name in the world

THE BEST THING ABOUT THIS FACT is that no one who wheels it out ever manages to actually remember the official name. And so, without further ado, here it is: *Al-Jamahiriyah al-'Arabiyah al-Libiyah ash-Sha'biyah al-Ishtirakiyah al-Uzma*.

Like any transliteration from Arabic, there are different versions with different spellings, but you get the idea: it's very long. In English, this is usually rendered as The Great Socialist People's Libyan Arab *Jamahiriyah*, with the last part being left in Arabic because it's a made-up word. Coined by Libyan leader Colonel Gadaffi, it approximates to 'state of the masses', and is intended to denote a form of state governed by the people. It is questionable whether all Libyan citizens would agree with this portrayal of what some outsiders might view as a military dictatorship.

Method of government aside, Libya wins hands-down when it comes to the number of letters in its official title. Coming a close second and third are Algeria (*Al-Jumhuriyah al-Jaza'iriyah ad-Dimuqratiyah ash-Sha'biyah*) and the United Kingdom of Great Britain and Northern Ireland.

There's a bit more competition when it comes to the shortest country name, with at least twelve countries comprising four-letter words (Chad, Cuba, Fiji, Guam, Iran, Iraq, Laos, Mali, Niue, Oman, Peru and Togo). But when you take into account official titles like 'The Democratic Republic of ...' the whole exercise self-implodes with pointlessness.

VERDICT: TRUE

But very boring.

There's an underground power station beneath Leicester Square, and the entrance is concealed as a half-price theatre ticket kiosk

UNTIL COMPARATIVELY RECENTLY there were several coal-fired and oil-fired power stations in central London, such as Battersea (which did not fully cease operation until 1983), Bankside (decommissioned in 1981 and now the Tate Modern art gallery) and Lots Road in Chelsea (which generated power for the London Underground until 2002). But what sort of power station could be contained underneath Leicester Square in the heart of the West End? Wouldn't hapless tourists be enveloped in billowing smoke or steam? There couldn't possibly be some sort of hydro-electric system going on – it would get in the way of the Piccadilly Line – and you couldn't put a wind farm underground. Perhaps there's a nuclear reactor that 'they' have not told anyone about: that might explain the secret use of the half-price theatre ticket kiosk.

Underneath that ticket kiosk (which has had its vowels and capitals pruned and is now called 'tkts' for no obvious reason), there is in fact an electricity substation. So it's not a power station in the sense of electricity generation, but it is the main facility to transform power from the National Grid for use in London's West End. The ticket kiosk isn't exactly the 'secret entrance' (there is a secret trapdoor nearby) but it does double as a secret ventilation system.

The substation was completed in 1991 and is on three levels: an entrance hall, the main transformer area, and a cabling level that is linked by a mile-long tunnel to another substation at Duke Street, near Grosvenor Square.

VERDICT: ALMOST

Until 1999 there was a nuclear reactor called JASON inside Christopher Wren's King William Building at the Royal Naval College in Greenwich; 'they' didn't publicise it much.

There's some place in Edinburgh where if you spit it's lucky

IF YOU'RE GOING to come up with a pub fact, it's important to keep it as vague as possible. The last thing you want is for someone to be able to pin you down on anything specific that could actually be challenged. This example is outstandingly useless – which is curious, because it's actually true, so there is no need for its author to hide behind a lack of substance and a haze of fuzzy grammar. The most likely explanation is that whoever first started recounting it had been to Edinburgh on a stag weekend, did some nominal sightseeing for one hour on the Sunday morning, and then got the train home with little or no recollection of where they'd actually visited or spat.

The 'some place' in question is the Heart of Midlothian, a rather unimposing heart-shaped pattern of cobbles near the High Kirk of St Giles in the Royal Mile. The mosaic marks the spot of the Edinburgh Tolbooth, built as (you guessed it) a toll booth, but later a prison and the scene of numerous executions. The Heart of Midlothian (which also gave its name to Hearts football club) was popularised as the name for the Tolbooth by Walter Scott, whose novel *Tales of My Landlord* (Second Series) – now known as *The Heart of Midlothian* – was published in 1818, a year after the prison's demolition. Scott originally wrote his novel under the pseudonym of Jedediah Cleishbotham, Schoolmaster and Parish-clerk of Gandercleugh.

It's said that prisoners used to spit on their way in for good luck, which is why this charming tradition is carried on by some passers-by today.

VERDICT: TRUE

The Heart is no longer actually in Midlothian, since Edinburgh became a separate authority in 1974.

The Portuguese word for 'turkey' is 'peru'

'TURKEY' IS AN ENGLISH WORD with very confused origins. To cut a long story short, the country is named after its people, the Turks, while the bird is probably so called because of its associations with Turkish importers in the 1500s. In fact, the word originally referred to the African guinea fowl, while the bird we today know as a turkey (*Meleagris gallopavo*) was mistakenly thought to be a species of guinea fowl and was given the same name. Neither bird is native to the country of Turkey – *Meleagris gallopavo* originates from North America.

If this seems baffling, consider that the Turkish word for 'turkey' is *hindi* – which means 'from India'. As does the French term *dinde*, a corruption of *d'Inde*; while the Dutch word *kalkoen* and the Finnish word *kalkkuna* suggest a further pinpointing of the Indian origin of the bird to Calicut. (Just to confuse matters further, the Keralan city of Calicut is also known by its Malayam name, Kozhikode.)

Why did some Europeans assume the bird came from India rather than North America or Turkey? Perhaps because, in those days, India was identified with 'the exotic'. Most perplexingly of all, the modern-day turkey was introduced to India by the Portuguese, in whose language, yes, the word *peru* denotes a turkey. It's thought that the bird gained popularity in Portugal in the sixteenth century, not long after the conquest of Peru, and so the Portuguese believed it to have come from that country.

VERDICT: BEWILDERINGLY TRUE

As a final note on the matter, in Scots Gaelic the bird is called *cearc frangais*, meaning 'French chicken'.

Pier 39 is the most visited tourist attraction in the USA

Have you even heard of Pier 39? It's hardly as iconic as the Empire State Building, Mount Rushmore or the Golden Gate Bridge – which is not far from Pier 39 in San Francisco. However, if you've visited the city then you'll know what Pier 39 is: a renovated cargo pier housing a complex of shops, restaurants, amusement arcades and a carousel. The pier showcases performances by jugglers and magicians (but thankfully not those silver-painted statue-idiots who think that *standing still* constitutes entertainment), and affords excellent views of the Bay and the large numbers of sea lions that loll about in the West Marina.

Since there are no tickets and no turnstiles, exact numbers aren't known, but research has indicated that Pier 39 attracts a staggering 11 million visitors a year. However, according to the International Association of Amusement Parks and Attractions, in 2005 the Magic Kingdom at Florida's Walt Disney World was the most visited amusement park on the planet, attracting 16.2 million overexcited children and masochistic parents. So while Pier 39 is high on the list of the most visited attractions in the USA, it doesn't take top spot. Nevertheless, they can console themselves with the fact that Pier 39 has twice been voted 'San Francisco's best place to people watch' in the *San Francisco Chronicle*'s Readers' Choice poll.

VERDICT: FALSE

If you were to include the rest of Fisherman's Wharf and the surrounding area then you might be looking at America's most visited 'group of attractions', since this would automatically count all visitors to Alcatraz (whether or not they decide to swing by Pier 39 while waiting for the ferry from Pier 41), as well as tourists stopping at one of the many waterfront restaurants or being mildly disappointed by Ghirardelli Square.

The Pope's representative in China is called Cardinal Sin

THIS IS NOT TRUE, but until 2003 it was only incorrect with regard to the tiny matter of geography, for there was a Cardinal Sin in charge of the Catholic Church in the Philippines.

Jaime Sin was born in 1928 and worked his way up the ranks to become the Archbishop of Manila in 1974. Two years later Pope Paul VI promoted him to the College of Cardinals (this is a group of people who choose each new Pope, *not* a low-budget comedy starring Steve Guttenberg). He remained Archbishop of Manila until his retirement in 2003, when he was replaced by the less entertainingly named Gaudencio Borbon Rosales; after a period of ill health Jaime Sin died in 2005. During his time in office he was closely associated with the 'people power' movement to oust the corrupt President Marcos.

The Cardinal was noted for his dry wit, and was certainly amused by sounding like one of the seven deadly sins. He used to frequently welcome English-speaking visitors with the phrase 'welcome to the house of Sin' and quipped that the Church could never possibly appoint a 'Cardinal Sin'. Although presumably his followers quickly tired of hearing the same gags over and over again.

VERDICT: FALSE

The claim that Cardinal Sin was based in China is probably because Sin sounds like a Chinese name – which is in fact the case, as he did have Chinese ancestry on his father's side.

Disney World has the world's fifth biggest navy

FLORIDA'S WALT DISNEY WORLD RESORT is the largest theme park on earth, covering an area twice the size of Manhattan – plenty of territory to defend. But before you imagine Mickey Mouse torpedoing Cuban gunboats, remember that although the word 'navy' normally refers to military vessels, it can generally refer to any fleet, such as the merchant navy.

The size of Disney World – comprising the Magic Kingdom, Epcot, Disney–MGM Studios and the Animal Kingdom, as well as six golf courses, a car racetrack and over 30 hotels – means that effective transport links are essential. In addition to twelve monorail trains, over 160 buses, 28 trams, numerous other transport gizmos and a privately operated taxi service, the resort is home to over 750 waterborne craft of various sizes: ferries, shuttle boats, speedboats, canopy boats, sailing boats, rowing boats, pedal-powered boats and, if they count as boats, canoes.

The US Navy, the world's biggest, has something in the region of 250 ships, while China has around 200. But when it comes to countries' military strength, we're talking about aircraft carriers, frigates, destroyers, cruisers, command ships, submarines and support ships – not dinghies, banana boats and Goofy pedalos.

So although Disney World staff, or 'cast members', cheerfully trot out this 'fact' – sometimes it's the fourth, sixth or seventh biggest navy, depending who you talk to – it really doesn't mean anything.

VERDICT: FALSE
Until Disney World shut down its 20,000 Leagues Under the Sea

ride in 1994, followed by the 1998 closure of the similar Submarine Voyage ride at Disneyland in California, Disney also claimed to have the eighth largest submarine fleet in the world; this may be the source of the original publicity claim.

There's a pub in London that is technically in Cambridgeshire

DUE TO A HISTORICAL ODDITY, this was actually true at one time, despite the fact that the county of Cambridgeshire is about 65 kilometres (40 miles) from the outskirts of London. The pub in question, The Olde Mitre, is on Ely Court, an alleyway near Holborn Circus between Ely Place and Hatton Garden.

Until the late eighteenth century the Bishops of Ely – the nearest cathedral city to Cambridge – had their London residence in Ely Place, where they built Ely House and the adjacent St Ethelreda's Church. Sadly, the glory days – when residents were not subject to taxation, and the pub's licence was administered by Cambridgeshire county council – are over: the bishops moved out in the 1770s, when most of the present buildings were constructed, and Ely Place is now administered as a private road by the Commissioners of Ely Place.

Ely Place has a team of two beadles, technically a 'police force' (see p. 266), who, according to lore, have to grant the Metropolitan Police permission to enter. In reality, however, while the beadles are in charge of all the goings-on in the street, the Met won't hang around for an invite if they're in hot pursuit of a swag-carrying criminal.

VERDICT: TIME, GENTLEMEN, PLEASE

There has been a boozer on the site since about 1546, though it was rebuilt in 1772 (perhaps the first one should have been The *Really* Olde Mitre); the pub still trades heavily on its Cambridgeshire credentials.

In all hotel rooms, if you examine the chest of drawers, you will find a pornographic magazine sellotaped to the underside of the bottom drawer

THIS IS SO EASILY DISPROVED that it's amazing it has entered common belief in any form. Anyone claiming this is surely aware of how untrue it must be – but continues to spread the word because they are so amused by the thought of a porn equivalent of the Gideons International, with volunteers dutifully taping jazz mags to hotel furniture throughout the world in the hope of providing 'spiritual relief' to bored businessmen.

Many 'surveys' have been conducted over the years about the weird things left behind in hotel rooms. These 'studies' inevitably prove to be lazy and one-dimensional publicity devices for hotel chains and travel companies, who will make up any old nonsense (gorilla suits, artificial legs, stuffed animals, grandfather clocks, etc.) so that the company's name will be obediently reported in the 'news' by lazy and one-dimensional journalists.

As for things *deliberately* left behind in hotel rooms, the statistics are sparse – although a lazy and one-dimensional survey for a travel website in 2003 reported that Gideon Bibles were rated as the least useful item for business travellers, while only 2 per cent of respondents rated 'adult TV channels' as the most useful. If this were a representative survey – which it isn't – it would be possible to conclude that there's not much demand for sub-furniture pornography either.

VERDICT: RIDICULOUS

Not a lot else you can say, really.

Grantham was once voted the most boring town in Britain

ONCE? *Only once?* It seems hard to believe, doesn't it? Well, many people claim that Grantham has been awarded the 'most boring town' accolade twice or more in the last quarter of a century, but the vote that made the place forever synonymous with tedium was a listeners' poll on BBC Radio 1 in 1981.

The tiresome Lincolnshire town had never been particularly well known – for boredom or anything else – until the appearance of Margaret 'milk-snatcher' Thatcher, against whom the Radio 1 listeners may have been rebelling: the ex-prime minister, born in Grantham, and apple-bumping scientist Isaac Newton, who went to school there, are probably the best-known figures associated with the town.

In 1981 there was nothing to do in Grantham except turn to one of its many sub-standard pubs. Of course, times have changed. The humdrum market town – whose cultural highlights include two shopping centres and a branch of Ask Pizza where Barry

Manilow is rumoured to have eaten – has now become so tedious that a large number of its inhabitants have turned from alcohol to heroin as a way of passing the time. Even the semi-legendary drinking establishment Dr Thirsty's has now shut down due to a dearth of alcoholics.

It is perhaps astonishing that Grantham did not appear at all in *The Idler* magazine's 2003 book of *Crap Towns*, or its 2004 sequel. This is probably due to a technicality whereby 'crap' relates to more criteria than simply 'boring'.

VERDICT: NOT TRUE ENOUGH

Should you wish to help reverse the town's image and pay it a visit, Grantham's official website is at www.grantham-online. co.uk; you may also find www.samaritans.org useful.

No one has ever met anyone who's been to an Aberdeen or Angus Steak House

THIS IS A 'FACT' THAT may be specific to London, where Aberdeen and Angus Steak Houses are a familiar and intriguing sight throughout the West End. They have long been regarded as a place that tourists visit – but that residents of the capital wouldn't touch even with an antiseptically treated, 20-foot barge pole, at least not since the 1970s. So the claim probably originates in Londoners' bemusement as to why on earth tourists continue to eat at the steak houses in question.

At one point, in fact, even the tourists gave them a wide berth. In October 2002 the Aberdeen Steak House group – which operated numerous food outlets including Angus Steak Houses, Maxine's Brasseries and the American Café Bistro – went into receivership and had to sell off the restaurants, following several problematic years spanning Mad Cow Disease, the foot-and-mouth crisis, and the downturn in tourism following September 11. Subsequently, however, the majority shareholder, the reclusive Ali Salih, has started buying back some of the outlets, to create a distinctive new chain of restaurants called, er, the Scotch Steak House Group.

In March 2003 the journalist Quentin Letts visited one of the restaurants for the *Daily Mail* and reported that the food was retro but good. Someone must have met Quentin Letts, even if no one is likely to own up to it, so the claim is disproved.

VERDICT: FALSE

When reading restaurant reviews, don't forget that one man's abusive service is another man's humiliation fantasy.

There are no female architects

JAMES BROWN SANG ABOUT HOW this is a man's, man's, man's world, and although it's unlikely he had the architecture profession in mind, it's certainly not a field in which women get much coverage. All you ever hear about is Richard Rogers this, Norman Foster that, Daniel Libeskind went off in a huff, and so on.

Clearly some architects are women. To name just three, for debunking purposes: Julia Morgan, who designed William Randolph Hearst's castle; Zaha Hadid, the first (and so far only) female winner of the Pritzker Architecture Prize; and Christine Hawley, Chair of London's Bartlett Faculty of the Built Environment. But it has long been recognised that women's representation within the profession is woefully lacking. The specific problem is women moving to other fields after they finish studying architecture.

Studies in the US, UK and Australia have found the proportion of female architecture students to be between 35 and 50 per cent; but only between 1 and 10 per cent of partners, principals or directors of architecture firms are women. A 2003 study undertaken for the Royal Institute of British Architects concluded: 'The gradual erosion of confidence and de-skilling caused by the lack of creative opportunities for female architects, sidelining, limited investment in training, job insecurity and low pay, led to reduced self-esteem and poor job satisfaction in architectural practice.' So just a couple of issues to address, then.

Elizabeth Wilbraham, née Mytton, has been cited as the world's first female architect. She designed the present house at Weston Park in Shropshire in 1671, and her plans for restoring the nearby St Andrew's Church in 1700 are possibly the oldest surviving architectural designs drafted by a woman.

VERDICT: FALSE

James Brown also sang about having ants in his pants and getting on the good foot – possibly due to the aforementioned ants.

There are no trees in Iceland

ASSUMING THIS FACT RELATES TO the island republic in the Atlantic Ocean rather than the UK-based supermarket chain of the same name (which has been known to stock Christmas trees), it's a pretty bold claim, since it should be easy for anyone who's been there to spot a tree. But with a total population of around 300,000 and a fairly isolated location, relatively few people have actually been there in comparison with similarly sized European countries such as England or Portugal.

While trees do exist in Iceland (Akureyri, for example, is noted for its rowans), they are very scarce – but there used to be plenty. In fact, the Icelandic sagas tell of an island completely covered with forest, although admittedly the sagas aren't conclusive proof of anything. The deforestation isn't purely to do with the cold climate, the volcanic activity or grazing sheep; these are just three of the factors that have prevented trees growing back after they were chopped down by human settlers, who needed to build houses and fuel fires.

The scarcity of trees has a number of knock-on effects. Lack of cover makes for some very windy locations, and the island tends to attract birds that prefer cliffs to branches when it comes to nesting. Worse still, Iceland's paintballing industry has been wiped out, which in turn has had a devastating effect on the country's workforce, who now lack essential team-building skills.

After reaching near-extinction in the twentieth century, trees – such as birch, mountain ash and pines – are making a comeback at an astonishing rate. According to the country's tourist board,

Iceland plants more trees per head of population than any other country in the world.

VERDICT: FALSE
In 2005 the supermarket chain Iceland was bought by Baugur – an Icelandic company.

Burlington Arcade has its own police force

BURLINGTON ARCADE REPRESENTS, according to the official website at least, 'the height of stylish shopping in London's West End'. Connecting Piccadilly with Burlington Gardens, it is a picturesque Regency-style arcade of shops – or, one should probably say, boutiques. In other words, it's the sort of place you would buy a Fabergé egg rather than a pickled one.

The architect Samuel Ware designed the covered arcade for Lord George Cavendish of the adjacent Burlington House (now home to the Royal Academy of Arts); it opened for business in 1819 and its owner intended from the outset to keep out the riff-raff.

The 'force' in question consists of a group of smartly uniformed beadles, who to this day enforce a number of strict rules laid down by Lord Cavendish. The rules can be summarised as follows:

NO SINGING – NO OPEN UMBRELLAS
NO HUMMING – NO LARGE PARCELS
NO WHISTLING – NO MAKING MERRY
NO BEGGING – NO HURRYING

To describe these beadles as 'police' is just about acceptable. To quote one of the definitions provided by the *Oxford English*

Dictionary, for example, 'police' can refer to 'any body of men, officially instituted or employed to keep order' or to 'enforce regulations'.

VERDICT: TRUE

As far as can be ascertained, the beadles don't have any strong feelings about yodelling, parasols or heavy petting.

There are more guns than voters in Texas

THE POPULATION OF TEXAS is over 20 million, but the number of people eligible to vote – in other words, the population minus children, visitors and other timewasters – was around 13.8 million at the time of the 2004 election. The number of *voters*, however, was half that number, with an official turnout of 51 per cent.

So for this claim to be true, there would need to be something in the order of 6.8 million firearms kicking around the Lone Star State. That seems pretty extraordinary, until you realise that gun owner-ship seems to be a source of pride and political clout in Texas. In 2002, for example, when John Sharp ran for Lieutenant Governor, he said in an interview with the *Dallas Morning News* that he was the proud owner of 30 rifles and shotguns and 'a couple of pistols'. If this was indicative of the general level of gun ownership among voters – and bear in mind that John Sharp is a *Democrat* – we'd be looking at something like 200 million firearms.

It's probably not quite that extensive. Successive polls have indicated that around 50 per cent of all households have at least one gun. Texas has around 7.4 million occupied households, so if half of them had just one firearm, that would be 3.7 million. However, the figure is believed to be far higher, with official estimates regularly putting the number of firearms in Texas at nearly 70 million. It seems then, that many Texans must own so many guns that finding them lodged down the back of the sofa and accidentally putting them in the wash in their jeans pockets must be commonplace. In fact, whenever they misplace one, they probably just buy another rather than being arsed to look for it.

VERDICT: TRUE

In 2005 Houston police felt compelled to run a campaign discouraging locals from participating in the tinpot New Year tradition of firing guns into the air.

There's a book called *Pub Knitting*

THERE IS INDEED – and it's about designs you can create over a beer with your mates, rather than a guide to knitting your own pub. If you've not seen it in your local bookshop, that's probably because it's only available through Rowan Yarns: the author, Rachel Henderson, is an Edinburgh-based design consultant for the knitwear company.

Pub Knitting contains patterns for fourteen 'streetwear accessories', such as a beer cosy and a holder for your MP3 player, interspersed with some rather entertaining photos of Rachel Henderson's knit-buddies. Overall the book is an intriguing attempt to bring knitting to a wider audience (or to put it more cynically: to get people to buy more wool from Rowan).

A similar goal, arguably a more specifically 'post-feminist' one, is shared by the series of *Stitch 'n Bitch* books by the American author and *Bust* magazine editor Debbie Stoller. (The missing final apostrophe on *'n* has no doubt given Lynne Truss many a sleepless night.) And plenty of other recent books, such as Lily Chin's *The Urban Knitter* and Rachael Matthews' *Knitorama* – which features an apple protector, a woolly hand grenade and a crocheted pint of stout – have been best-sellers. Whilst these aren't limited to extreme knitting in drinking establishments, they have helped fuel the recent surge in the craft's popularity, as demonstrated by the number of celebrities spotted knitting in public, such as Winona Ryder, Russell Crowe and Madonna. Of course, by the time Madonna is seen doing something, you know that the bandwagon in question has long ago run out of fuel, swerved off the road and careered into an open sewer.

VERDICT: TRUE
Drinking while knitting should be undertaken in moderation – otherwise it can become a case of 'knit one, hurl one'.

Parts of Canada used to be in Louisiana

LOOKING AT A MAP OF North America, this claim does seem rather improbable, given that Louisiana, a state located on the Gulf of Mexico, is over 1,600 kilometres (1,000 miles) away from the southern Canadian border, a distance covered by four or five other states (depending which part of Canada the crow is flying to). So was the state of Louisiana once really that big? Did it cover an area the size of Europe; or was it perhaps very long and very thin – like a motorway, but with its own legal system? Or did 'parts of Canada' find their way onto the back of a pickup truck and get accidentally transported down south, only to be returned when the mistake was discovered?

Well, it's more to do with the fact that the name Louisiana eventually came to denote only one small area – the southern tip – of a vast region of the same name, which covered all or parts of the modern-day states of Arkansas, Texas, New Mexico, Oklahoma!, Kansas, Missouri, Colorado, Nebraska, Iowa, Wyoming, North and South Dakota, Minnesota and Montana. (Sorry: Oklahoma! just never looks right without the exclamation mark.) And it *just about* stretched into the very southern areas of Alberta, Saskatchewan and Manitoba in what's now known as Canada.

This region was first named and claimed in 1682 by the French explorer René Robert Cavalier de la Salle, to honour King Louis XIV (not the previous thirteen kings of the same name, lest there be any confusion). After the French lost it to the British and the Spanish, the Spanish secretly signed the western part back over to the French – who promptly sold the whole lot to the fledgling United States. Those were the days!

VERDICT: TRUE

Oh, and in 1818, under the Anglo–American convention, Britain got the bits at the top, which subsequently formed part of the independent nation of Canada.

Underneath Cleopatra's Needle is a time capsule containing Victorian pornography

THE EGYPTIAN MONUMENT that now stands next to the Thames in London was originally erected in Heliopolis in the fifteenth century BC, before being moved to Alexandria in Roman times. In the nineteenth century AD, in a classic example of colonial generosity, the monument was 'gifted' to the British – not by the Egyptians, but by the Turkish viceroy.

The obelisk was transported to London by sea in an iron cylinder that was temporarily lost during a storm in the Bay of Biscay. It was positioned – after much debate – on the brand-new Victoria Embankment, and was finally lowered into place on 12 September 1878.

The trailblazing Egyptologist E.A. Wallis Budge, in *Cleopatra's Needles and Other Egyptian Obelisks* (1926), describes a collection of objects buried beneath the monument that is so extensive and bizarre you'd think they were sending it off to an alien planet: a complete set of British currency 'and a rupee'; weights and measures; a portrait of Queen Victoria; documents about the transporting of the obelisk to London and associated lifting equipment; a translation of the gospel of John 3:16 ('For God so loved the world, that he gave his only begotten son') in a staggering 215 languages; the book of Genesis in Arabic; the Pentateuch in Hebrew; Whitaker's *Almanack*; Bradshaw's *Railway Guide*; a map of London; a selection of newspapers; a razor; a box of cigars and some pipes; a feeding bottle; a collection of toys; women's toiletries; and, in the manner of the miniature model of the factory 'that makes miniature models of factories' in *Austin Powers*, a bronze scale model of the obelisk itself. Last but not least, the time capsule includes 'photographs of twelve pretty Englishwomen'.

This latter inclusion is presumably the basis of the porn theory. Sadly, however, we don't know who the pretty Englishwomen were, or who was involved in judging them pretty. While there is no evidence to suggest that the photographs were anything more than genteel portraits, the only sure-fire way to prove or disprove this claim would be to dig up the needle.

VERDICT: TITILLATING BUT UNLIKELY

E.A. Wallis Budge could have made up this whole inventory, for all we know: the British Museum, his former employer, today warns against the 'basic errors of fact and methodology' prevalent in his 'unreliable, and usually misleading' books.

The entire population of Liechtenstein could fit into Old Trafford twice

IT'S SAFE TO ASSUME THAT this factistic means that the seating capacity of the giant Manchester stadium is double the population of the dwarfish European principality – rather than suggesting that everyone in Liechtenstein could fit into Old Trafford, walk out again, and then re-enter for a second sitting, before getting bored and refusing to do so a third time. Equally one assumes that 'fit' means to occupy the terraces and other accommodation, rather than getting Liechtensteiners to pile on top of each other on the pitch, filling up the space to the top of the stadium's roof like some sort of 1950s student prank.

In which case, this should be pretty easy to determine. In July 2005 the population of Liechtenstein, according to the *CIA World Factbook*, was estimated to be 33,717. (It is a truth universally acknowledged that the CIA always know more about any country than that country's government, including the USA's.) And the capacity of Old Trafford, according to the Football Association, is 68,174. Therefore the population of Liechtenstein could fit into Old Trafford 2.02 times.

On 29 March 2003, during the qualifying rounds for Euro 2004, England had to play Liechtenstein at the Rheinpark stadium in Vaduz, with an attendance of 3,548. The most notable event of the match was the singing of the national anthems, as Liechtenstein's anthem shares the same melody as 'God Save the Queen'. At least they saved money on the band.

VERDICT: TRUE
If laid end to end, the entire population of Liechtenstein would stretch from central London to Stansted airport.

The Irish for 'Blackpool' is 'Dublin'

THIS IS A SLIGHTLY MUDDLED historical claim, but is basically correct, if approached the other way round – in other words, it might make slightly more sense to say that the English for 'Dublin' is 'Blackpool'.

In the English language the name used for the capital of the Republic of Ireland is a corruption of the Gaelic words *dubh* and *linn*, meaning 'black' and 'pool' respectively. So in this sense the city was indeed originally called 'black pool', apparently a reference to the darkness of the river Liffey.

This is not to say, however, that the Lancashire city of Blackpool is referred to by Gaelic speakers as 'Dublin'. To the contrary, they refer to it as 'that place on Morecambe Bay with the mini Eiffel Tower and the dodgy wooden roller-coaster, and which keeps the likes of Bobby Davro in business'.

The Gaelic name for the capital, meanwhile, is no longer Dubh Linn but Baile Átha Cliath, which means 'town of the hurdle ford', a name evoking the historical means of crossing the Liffey.

VERDICT: TRUER WHEN SPOKEN THAN WHEN WRITTEN DOWN

Note: Bobby Davro has a thriving career, not just in Blackpool, and excelled alongside Melinda Messenger in the 2005–6 season of *Aladdin* at Woking's New Victoria Theatre.

The town of Levan is the word 'navel' backwards, because it's in the centre of Utah

THE SMALL TOWN of Levan is about 100 miles south of Salt Lake City, so it's certainly in the centre of Utah. But whether the Juab County town was deliberately given the name 'navel' backwards is questionable, to say the least.

The only thing that seems absolutely certain is that the town was named in 1867 by Brigham Young, the second prophet of the Church of Jesus Christ of Latter-day Saints, who was responsible for the establishment of the Mormons in Utah (which used to be part of Mexico). Given that Young founded numerous other settlements with rather more literal names, such as Cedar City (originally called Little Muddy, and then Coal Creek), and was not known for his light-hearted pranks, there is no reason why he would have reversed the word.

Historical documents show several different spellings, so the 'navel' theory can be discounted. Possible French and Paiute etymologies indicate the word could have meant sunrise, frontier settlement, little water or the rear section of a moving army, but there is no definite evidence of Young's intentions. However, it's much more likely that Levan was, like so many settlements in the New World, named after a person. For example, there's a Levan in Jackson County, Illinois (nowhere near the centre of the state, incidentally), named after a farmer called Samuel Levan.

There was an Irish Saint Levan who supposedly split a large rock in two with a staff. Perhaps Brigham Young, the 'American Moses', was inspired by the whole parting with a staff concept. But while he wasn't averse to naming a town after a saint (Saint George, in south-west Utah, being an example), Levan was a relatively obscure saint operating out of Cornwall, so it's an unlikely source – and why omit the 'Saint' part? Likewise, Levan was the name of several prominent Georgians of the Dadiani dynasty; but that's Georgia in the Caucasus, rather than Georgia 'on my mind' in the American South, so again, it's not very plausible. Even more improbable as a source is the town of Levan in Albania, home to the country's oldest Roma community.

Ultimately the most likely origin would have been a descendant of the Levan family (originally Le Van or LeVan), Huguenots who left Normandy for Pennsylvania, by way of the Netherlands.

VERDICT: NAVEL-GAZING

In 1869 Brigham Young opened America's first incorporated department store.

The Korean national anthem is 'Auld Lang Syne'

IN MANY COUNTRIES 'Auld Lang Syne' is traditionally associated with New Year's Eve, or Hogmanay in its birthplace of Scotland, where it is also sung at the end of Burns Night. For most people, singing 'Auld Lang Syne' means crossing your arms to hold the hands of the people next to you, hollering the opening words 'Should auld acquaintance be forgot' and then drunkenly mumbling the rest until you realise that it really does go on a bit, and that somewhere in the kitchen there must lurk at least one remaining can from the four-pack you so generously brought earlier in the evening.

It's the Scots poet Robert Burns whom we have to thank for 'Auld Lang Syne', although its exact origins are shrouded in folk-loric mystery. He claimed to be the first to write down the song, making various additions and amendments, although similar poems existed previously. The words were first published in 1796 after his death, while the original melody has long since been forgotten. The tune known as 'Auld Lang Syne' today was published together with the words in 1799, though musically it is believed to derive from an earlier song such as 'The Miller's Wedding'.

In Korea the national anthem, 'Aegukga', *used to be* sung to the melody of 'Auld Lang Syne' until the end of the Second World War (although the anthem was officially banned under the

Japanese occupation from 1910). When the country was split in two, South Korea adopted a new melody that had been written in the 1930s by Ahn Eak-tae, while North Korea created an all-new anthem with its own words and music.

VERDICT: FALSE
Until 1972 the 'Auld Lang Syne' melody was also used for the national anthem of the Maldives.

There's only one cash machine in Albania

THE REPUBLIC OF ALBANIA, sandwiched against the Adriatic and Ionian seas by Serbia and Montenegro, Macedonia and Greece, is one of Europe's poorest countries, still trying fully to escape the legacy of Enver Hoxha's brand of Communism and become a stable democracy with a viable economy. In 1997 Albanian society nearly broke down due to a belief in pyramid selling as a successful means to make money.

Credit cards are not widely accepted in Albania. Although this is gradually changing as banks establish a bigger network of point-of-sale systems, the current advice is still to convert your money into Albanian currency – the lek – at a bank or legitimate bureau de change, and then deal solely in cash.

The cash machine, ATM or 'hole in the wall' is a relatively recent invention – the first in the world was installed in 1967 by Barclays Bank in Enfield, north London – so it's understandable that coverage in Albania would be minimal. Logically, at some stage it must have been true that there was only one cash dispenser in the country (unless the first two were installed simultaneously) but although some guidebooks still claim the 'one ATM' fact, it's no longer true. For example, the American Bank of Albania, backed by the not-for-profit Albanian–American Enterprise Fund, has over twenty cash machines throughout the country, all of which accept MasterCard and Visa. ProCredit Bank has around the same number, while Raiffeisen Bank, the country's largest, can lay claim to a network of around 100 cash machines.

VERDICT: FALSE

The continent of Antarctica also has its own cash machine: a Wells Fargo ATM at McMurdo Station, which, pleasingly, does not charge a fee.

Apparently it's a myth that you can see the Great Wall of China from space

ANY STATEMENT THAT STARTS with the words 'apparently it's a myth' is always going to be pretty shaky. But this one is intriguing because it serves to negate an otherwise established claim. The 'fact' about the Great Wall of China's visibility from space has got so out of hand over the years that people are now cack-footedly stumbling over themselves trying to point out how untrue it is.

There are a number of Great Wall of China claims. Sometimes it's said to be the only man-made structure visible from the moon. (It would be noteworthy that this version of the claim pre-dates the first moon landings by several decades – except that apparently it's a myth that anyone has ever landed on the moon: everyone knows it was a Hollywood studio lot.) Sometimes it's the only man-made structure visible from 'outer space' with the naked eye. Sometimes it's just 'one of the few' man-made structures visible from space.

The wall certainly can't be seen with the unaided eye from the moon, but it has sometimes been visible to astronauts orbiting the earth. While it's very long (over 6,000 km, about 3,700 miles), it's also mostly very narrow and is pretty similar in colour to its surroundings, which means the wall is not as recognisable from space as the Giza pyramids. When the bumbling Chinese-American astronaut Leroy Chiao photographed the area from the International Space Station in 2004, he was not himself certain that he could see the wall – but the picture was subsequently confirmed as the first photograph of the wall from space.

VERDICT: FALSE
Apparently.

ACKNOWLEDGEMENTS

THIS BOOK WOULD NEVER HAVE seen the light of day without the advice, skill and vision of my marvellous editor, Sarah Lavelle, to whom I am deeply indebted – particularly for having to put up with my chronic inability to count. I extend my thanks to Tony Lyons and Nicky Barneby, whose excellent design perfectly complements the spirit of the book, as do Sarah Nayler's wonderful illustrations. Thanks also to Two Associates and NB Illustration for playing their part in making the visual aspects of the book come together; to James Sleigh for his overall guidance and invaluable suggestions; to Natalie Hunt and Henrietta Scott-Gall for keeping things running smoothly; to Vicki Vrint for her eagle-eyed proof-reading; and to Lisa Footitt for the all-important index.

I am grateful to the following individuals and institutions who took the time to assist me with research, no matter how trivial or nonsensical my questions may have been: The Bank of England's Public Information & Enquiries Group; Julie Brown (RecycleNow.com); Michael Bunyan (Environmental Statistics and Indicators, Defra); Ken Cochran (President of Jackson County Historical Society, Illinois); Peter Cochran and Maureen Crisp (The Byron Society); Boothby Graffoe and Ingrid Ricciardello

(Assembly Management); Richard Jardine (the Tower Bridge Exhibition); Rod Laird (Westminster City Council); Dave Lockyear (City of London Police); Ron Lodge (Lincolnshire Echo); Fred Long (Ely Place Beadle); Núria López Mercader (Centre de Recursos de Biodiversitat Animal, Facultat de Biologia, Universitat de Barcelona); The MIPT Terrorism Knowledge Base (www.tkb.org); Fleur Nixon (Crossrail); Elizabeth Scudder (London Metropolitan Archives); Karen Short (Nestlé UK); Craig Sperry (Recorder for Juab County, Utah); Linda Stratmann; Jhodi Ward (Royal Albert Hall); and Stephen Webb (Waste Watch).

Kate Pool and the Society of Authors were particularly helpful in matters relating to 'becoming a proper author'.

Thanks to those who provided moral or liquid assistance, suggested inclusions or amendments to the book, or who simply provided inspiration by being in the right pub at the wrong time: Ian Aspinall; Justine Bird; Katie Burrell; Mick Faver; Deborah Heath; Nick Kouppari; Lucie March; Lucy Reid; Patrick Rodger; Tim Rodger; Steve Russell; Allan Saunders ('The Phantom Menace'); Alan Thawley; Simon Turner (real name Peter Trait); Alex Ward; and Emma Ward (no relation).

Finally, I am especially grateful to the fantastic Karen Jeger, for her emotional and material support during a period that was for me very busy and for her very boring.

INDEX